THE DOVE AND THE BEAR

LUIGI FORNI

Translated by Tina Mattei

HIPPOCRENE BOOKS INC.

First published in USA by Hippocrene Books, Inc.
171 Madison Avenue, New York, NY 10016

Published in the UK by Midas Books
12 Dene Way, Speldhurst, Tunbridge Wells, Kent TN3 0NX

Text © Luigi Forni 1983

Translation © Tina Mattei 1983

ISBN 0-88254-833-6

All rights reserved. No part of this publication may be
reproduced, stored in a retrieval system, or transmitted,
in any form or by any means, electronic, mechanical, photo-
copying, recording or otherwise, without the prior permission
of Midas Books.

Printed in Great Britain

*To one
who knows
when to speak
and when
to keep silent*

Some Sayings

In the name of Marx

'Peace is what man, the worker, needs most of all, whether operating a machine tool, or a smelting furnace, whether driving a tractor or erecting a building, whether lecturing in a university auditorium or doing research in a laboratory.'

'Experience teaches us that for peace to become genuinely durable, it is necessary for statesmen and politicians to make consistent and purposeful efforts.'

'Now the world is entering a period when the task of translating the principles of peaceful coexistence and mutually beneficial cooperation into daily practical actions is coming to the fore.'

'This is a crucial period. Those to whom the destinies of states and peoples have been entrusted should show that their deeds match their words.'

(Public statements by Leonid Brezhnev)

In the name of God

'We see clearly that humanity is divided in a great many ways. The search for solutions that will permit human societies to carry out their own tasks and to live in justice is perhaps the main sign of our time.'

'We are aware that authentic dialogue cannot be easy, because it takes place between two concepts of the world which are diametrically opposed; but it must be possible and effective if the good of individuals and nations demands it.'

'We should always look for peace in the world first, and try to improve relationships and communications between all kind of people and political institutions. You must help yourselves and attack your problems and you will find improvement. You should never stop talking and discussing your problems. A solution will always come.'

'We must work for peace and reconciliation between the people and the nations of the whole world. We must try to come closer to one another. We must open the frontiers. When we are strong with the Spirit of God, we are also strong with faith in man.'

'Let your Spirit descend, and renew the face of the earth.'

(From the speeches of Pope John Paul II)

Prologue

I wish to describe how Pope John Paul II prevented the Polish crisis of 1980 from degenerating into the third world war. The circumstances which I am about to relate took place between December 1980 and January 1981, and are so extraordinary as to seem, at least in part, incredible. After the 1917 October Revolution in Russia neither a Catholic nor a Communist could have conceived the possibility that a Pontiff and a President of the Soviet Union would one day meet in secret to discuss the international situation. My reaction, when I first learned of such an extraordinary event, was therefore a mixture of scepticism and hilarity.

But my sources of information deserved the highest esteem and at least an attempt to verify the credibility of their story. On reflection, it made sense that an exceptional Pope had dared to expose himself to all kinds of dangers in the hope of averting further catastrophe for mankind.

Having accepted this theory, I was confronted with the arduous task of putting together the missing pieces of the mosaic, inserting episodes unknown to my readers into the framework of the daily activities of the Kremlin and of the Holy See at the time this historic encounter took place. It is of course not possible for me to reveal the contacts who enabled me to reach the conclusion that the meeting between John Paul II and Leonid Ilyich Brezhnev had really happened. In fact, in order to protect the identity of my informants I have deliberately altered some details of this narrative. And I have obviously 'reconstructed' the course of conversations; in the case of the discussions between the two protagonists, who faced each other with no witness, I have tried to remain faithful to the ideas that both had publicly expressed on other occasions. Nevertheless, I must ask forgiveness for having put words into their mouths.

The main objective of this book is to relate the content and the purpose of the dialogue that prevented the Red Army from invading Poland shortly after the birth of the independent trade union, Solidarity. Military intervention had already been prearranged down to the last detail, and zero hour fixed for between Christmas 1980 and 20 January 1981, the date of the beginning of the new American Administration with the inauguration of Ronald Reagan as President.

It would be erroneous to read this story as a sensational piece of reportage; to avoid such a risk, I have chosen to wait until now for publication. While praising the courageous action of the Holy Father, I want to give credit to the memory of his Soviet interlocutor for the initiative he took to safeguard and guarantee peace, even if on precarious terms. The explosive Polish crisis was defused when it had almost reached the point of no return. For this achievement we must be grateful not only to the Dove but also, just for once, to the Bear.

Rome

On the afternoon of Saturday 29 November 1980, a Soviet diplomat, aged around forty, showed his passport at the reception desk of the Excelsior Hotel in the Via Veneto and asked if a room had been reserved for him. He spoke in perfect English and smiled when the clerk, scanning the reservations' list, stopped his finger at the name indicated on the passport – Sergei Leonov. He was accompanied to a small suite of rooms on the third floor comprising a double bedroom with bath and a sitting room furnished with a divan, two armchairs, a low table and a television set. The boy who had carried his luggage assured Mr Leonov that the television functioned, pushing the buttons of the various channels.

'Anna Magnani,' murmured Leonov, as a scene from one of her old films, *Open City*, appeared on the screen.

'You know Magnani!' exclaimed the boy admiringly, before switching over to another station.

'She is famous all over the world,' replied Leonov, this time speaking in rather poor Italian.

'Shame she's dead,' commented the boy. He turned the set off and added: 'An actress like that is born only once in a lifetime.' He pocketed the tip offered, gave a slight bow, and went out.

Leonov had no time to spend watching Italian television. As soon as he was alone he read the instructions attached to the telephone, and learned that it was the direct dialling type. He did not touch the telephone, but opened his suitcase, taking out his clothes and hanging them neatly in the wardrobe. He showered quickly and dressed, putting on a fresh shirt and tie. From the four ties he had with him he selected one in blue decorated with yellow half-moons, which he fastened to his shirt with an ivory-headed pin, taking care that it pierced a half-moon. Checking in the mirror that all was in order, he descended to the street, declining with a nod the porter's offer of a taxi.

From the Via Veneto he turned into the Via Lombardia and walked slowly towards the Piazza di Spagna. Along the way he stopped at a public telephone and dialled a number of six digits. He let it ring four times without reply. He replaced the receiver and calmly redialled the number, as though he had made a mistake at the first attempt. He had no luck with the second call either. After the sixth ring he replaced the receiver with evident disappointment.

He reached the steps of Trinità dei Monti, having stopped to look with interest in the shop windows, especially those displaying the latest in men's fashion. Every so often he glanced with admiration at the façades of the buildings, and the balconies still ablaze with flowers even though winter had arrived. He stopped at a newspaper kiosk and read the headlines of the afternoon papers. The front pages were all dedicated to the recent earthquake which had devastated many regions of southern Italy. He started to descend the steps leading to the Piazza di Spagna. The air was extraordinarily mild, and sweet with the perfume of flowers. Young couples embraced on the steps, murmuring words of love.

Arriving in the piazza he stopped for a moment to admire the marble Barcaccia, a fountain which is a popular rendezvous of the Romans. He turned right towards the Babington, a favourite haunt of the bourgeoisie still faithful to the ritual of afternoon tea.

The first room was crowded and Leonov, looking around, directed himself towards the little room at the back. He sat at one of the few unoccupied tables, giving a slight nod of the head when a waiter asked if he would take tea. Did he prefer lemon or milk? 'Lemon,' he replied, somewhat vaguely.

A babble of noisy chatter buzzed about him. At a nearby table several ladies exchanged their impressions of a recent spring fashion show. 'Who could have thought that the mini skirt would come back into fashion?' asked a junoesque matron, nibbling daintily at a slice of apple pie. On the other side of the room an elderly gentleman caressed the hand of a young woman, stretching his arm across the table. She was crying silently and the man was whispering words of comfort to her. Perhaps he is going to leave her, thought Leonov. Then he noticed she was wearing black as though in mourning. He withdrew his attention and turned his eyes upon the prints adorning the walls. He had just swallowed the last of his tea when he received the signal he was waiting for.

A grizzle-haired man with half an unlighted cigar between his lips stood in the doorway. Their eyes met briefly; the newcomer looked about as though seeking a free table or some acquaintance. Not finding what he was looking for, the man turned back towards the exit. Before going out he took the cigar from his mouth and with exaggerated care placed it in the top pocket of his jacket.

Leonov quickly paid the bill and went out into the square. He crossed it at an angle to reach the Via della Croce, a street running parallel with the smart Via Condotti, and after a dozen or so paces stopped on the right under the signboard of a restaurant called 'da Otello'.

The day's menu hung in a frame outside. He was scanning the price when a voice behind him said in English: 'It is more expensive than last year.'

'Do you refer to some particular dish?' enquired Leonov.

'*Parmigiana di melanzane*,' the other replied. It was the same person who had appeared so briefly in the Babington.

'When I am in Rome I prefer to eat *ossobuco*,' Leonov said.

'Four plus six,' said the man. 'I have been waiting for your call since yesterday evening.' Together they strolled towards the Via del Corso.

Moscow

The Secretary-General of NATO, Joseph Luns, had denied in October 1980 that the invasion of Poland would automatically lead to the third world war. Replying to a direct question on the subject, Luns observed that Poland was not part of NATO and, therefore, the countries of the Atlantic Pact were not obliged to come to her defence in the unfortunate eventuality of Soviet aggression against Warsaw. 'It is not NATO's business,' he explained, 'to protect Poland from her so-called friends.' This statement was interpreted by part of international public opinion as an implicit 'warrant' from the West to the Soviet Union to march against Poland, repeating the bloody acts of 1968 in Czechoslovakia and of 1956 in Hungary.

The American Presidential election of 4 November 1980 introduced to the scene an imponderable factor in bringing Ronald Reagan to the White House. Barely twenty days had elapsed since the resounding victory of Reagan over Carter when an 'informative visit' of a private nature was made to Moscow by the American Senator Charles Percy, President designate of the new Senate Foreign Relations Committee.

Percy was received at the Kremlin on 26 November, and he brought a personal and confidential message from Reagan to Brezhnev which the Soviet Government immediately interpreted as a cold shower raining down on their audacious self-confidence.

The President elect communicated to Moscow that his Administration was not willing to give a free hand to the USSR in Polish internal affairs.

The Soviet as well as the Western Press reported the meeting between Brezhnev and Percy, limiting themselves to saying that the general perspectives of Soviet–American relations and of international relaxing of tension had been examined. Moscow newspapers underlined that Brezhnev had indicated to his visitor that the USSR was disposed towards 'friendly cooperation with Washington on an equal basis'. The Soviet news agency Tass added that Brezhnev had not omitted to stress to the American guest that the recent and 'serious deterioration in Soviet–American relations has had a very adverse effect on the general situation'.

Issuing from the meeting place, Percy stated that both parties had expressed 'their differences without equivocation'. Before leaving the USA, the Senator had consulted ex-Presidents Nixon and Ford. It must be inferred that the confidential message to Brezhnev, of which he was the bearer, resulted from and was agreed to in total by the entire leadership of the Republican Party.

The great importance attributed by Moscow to Reagan's warning, 'Take your hands off Poland', appeared to be implicitly confirmed by the fact that Percy was also received separately by both the Minister of Foreign Affairs, Andrei Gromyko, and the Soviet Defence Minister, Dmitri Ustinov. Listening repeatedly to the new American President's message, the Soviet leaders practically gave the impression of not wanting to believe their ears. The logic of Yalta, from where the partition of the world into two great counterpoised blocs was derived, had been repudiated – or at least placed in doubt – by the Americans.

After having evaluated, together with Gromyko and Ustinov, the gravity of the warning launched by Reagan, Brezhnev immediately convened a meeting of the Central Committee of the Communist Party to discuss its implications and possible consequences. The Russian leaders were faced with a risky dilemma: to take up Reagan's challenge and invade Poland or to submit to the conditions of the new Polish situation, judged by the 'hawks' of the Kremlin as the beginning of a dangerous fracture that could cause the collapse of the Socialist Alliance in Eastern Europe.

The chief ideologist, Michail Suslov, who had had a determining role in the fall of Khrushchev, proposed to his colleagues of the Central Committee a two-tiered strategy which would be the least dangerous to the Soviet Union. Firstly, the

15

Soviet Ambassador to Washington, Dobrynin, should be entrusted with 'hooking' Reagan to sound out his definite intentions regarding the possible military occupation of Poland. The second step, considered by Suslov to be even more important than the first, would take place in Rome – in the Vatican City. A means would have to be found to 'mobilize the Pope' so that he could personally exercise a braking influence on the rebellious Polish workers. Only if the second step failed, independently of the results of Dobrynin's mission in Washington, would the USSR have no alternative but to invade Poland.

After a long debate Suslov's proposal was put to the vote, and approved unanimously. The discussion, which took place within the walls of the Kremlin, firmly defined several points on which depended not only the immediate future of Poland but also that of the entire human race.

Russia felt fettered by the necessity of 'normalizing' the Polish situation with the greatest urgency, and preventing the development of a centrifugal movement that would rapidly extend to other satellite countries of Eastern Europe.

Western Kremlinologists understand perfectly the meaning, in Soviet phraseology, of 'normalization' in a socialist country: this very formula was invoked in Hungary in 1956 and in Czechoslovakia in 1968. Normalization means lining up the members of a 'brother party' who seem recalcitrant in carrying out Moscow's orders, recalling to obedience the governments of satellite nations, and subduing and severely punishing dissidents attempting to crack the solidarity of the Marxist-Leninist echelon. The recipe for normalization, as applied against the Hungarians and the Czechs, was codified in the 'Brezhnev Doctrine', according to which the Red Army and the military forces of the adherent countries of the Warsaw Pact are used to intervene repressively when a socialist member state of the Alliance is in danger from elements of the so-called counter-revolutionaries. It is of little importance, when it comes to military intervention, that the apparent counter-revolutionaries comprise the major part of the population, trying to shake off the yoke of the local Communist party and Soviet domination. During the 'Prague Spring', a joke went around which fully illustrated the significance of the fraternal aid the Soviet Union is always ready to provide to socialist countries in difficulty. The joke was coined in the form of a question: Which is the happiest country in the world? Answer: Israel, because she is not surrounded by brother countries.

The need for military intervention against Poland was subordinated by the Politburo of the USSR to the outcome of the Pope's mediation *in extremis* between the Communist regime and the independent trade union Solidarity, around which were clustered the nationalist aspirations and religious sentiments of a great majority of the Polish workers.

The initiative proposed by Suslov was enthusiastically seconded by Brezhnev for certain considerations, which the Soviet President illustrated before proceeding to the resultant unanimous vote. Brezhnev's arguments were based on a few incontrovertible facts. The Polish Pope could become a precious and irreplaceable ally for the pacification of the souls of his country of origin, whose practising Catholics comprised almost one hundred per cent of the population. The Soviet leader recalled to the attention of his Government that Poland had 6700 parishes, 14,000 churches and chapels managed by a total of 64 bishops, 15,000 priests and about 30,000 nuns. 'Each of these parishes, churches and chapels,' explained Brezhnev, 'could be used as a subversive den, organizing strikes, sabotage, and acts of passive resistance, not to mention religious-run schools and the three Catholic universities. These dens could become nests of armed resistance if our divisions marched on Warsaw.

'In Hungary in 1956, the Catholic counter-revolutionaries were led by Cardinal Mindszenty, a cowardly fanatic who voluntarily entrapped himself in the American Embassy. For Poland we can count Cardinal Wyszynski on one side and the Pope on the other. Old Wynszynski can be easily neutralized but Wojtyla, no – because he is free to move from outside. To win our battle without loss of blood we have, therefore, to recruit the Pope. To put him to the service of our socialist cause would be impossible; it is enough to show him clearly the catastrophe that would result from a frontal encounter between the Church and the Polish government.'

The Minister of Foreign Affairs, Gromyko, a participant in the deliberations of the Politburo, described Solidarity as a snarling dog that the Church held on a lead. 'When the master is away the dog barks,' he said. 'In this case we have to make master Wojtyla understand that the dog needs muzzling, as we cannot permit him to gnaw at the fruits of socialism. No affectionate master wants to see his dog beaten because it is too noisy.' This caused laughter among the audience.

At the end of the debate the Soviet leaders were agreed that the invasion of Poland should take place before 20 January 1981 if the attempts to avoid such an event failed. In that way the new American President would find himself, at his inauguration, confronted by a *fait accompli*.

Rome

'The Chief wants a detailed report by ten o'clock tomorrow morning. He is installed in the Ambassador's private residence,' said Leonov.

'I have brought the maps of the Vatican and of Castel Gandolfo, as agreed,' replied his companion. 'The Pope's habitual routes are marked in red.'

'Well done, Comrade Monsignore,' approved Leonov, pleased. 'We will study them at our ease. Are there any new pontifical journeys envisaged within the next few days? This Wojtyla travels faster than a sputnik and it is difficult to keep up with him.'

'After his visit to Germany he decided not to go abroad until the end of February, when there will be a trip to Pakistan, the Philippines, Guam and Japan.'

'Johnny Walker was a stay-at-home in comparison. What about State audiences?'

'He received Margaret Thatcher last Monday, and is now preparing to meet the Yugoslav President, Cviyetin Mijatovic, next month. In between there are the usual administrative duties, general audiences, the Sunday Angelus blessing in St Peter's Square, and so on . . .'

'I saw the photo of the meeting with Mrs Thatcher. The Iron Lady was dressed for the occasion like an ebony doll. Did they speak about Northern Ireland?'

'The hunger strike by members of the IRA in Belfast prisons was discussed. The Irish Church is pressing for the reform of the prison system and a countermeasure to hasten the end of the strike. Vatican opinion is that the Conservative Government will be compelled to give in.'

'Did they speak of Poland?'

'Casually. London is ready to join in any initiative of NATO against a hypothetical invasion, beginning with commercial sanctions.'

'It makes you laugh! They trifle with the blunt weapon of commercial sanctions only to fill their mouths with threats. Economic sanctions in the past have never worked, as the events in Afghanistan and Iran show. Do you remember, Comrade Monsignore, the time when Fascist Italy was threatened with economic sanctions after the invasion of Ethiopia? The Italian industrialists continued to make huge profits while Mussolini rubbed his hands in amusement.'

They had crossed the Piazza Augusto Imperatore and were heading towards the river. 'The Italian Vaticanists have written that the Tiber has become wider following the nomination of a Polish Pope. The reason is that Wojtyla, unlike his predecessors, doesn't like poking his nose in this country's internal affairs. Pius XII had to be consulted at every government crisis, even when it came to choosing new ministers,' said the Monsignore.

'We would prefer that Wojtyla dedicated himself to Italian affairs rather than to those of Poland,' commented Leonov. 'Why is he not advised to interest himself in the troubles of the Christian Democrats?'

'He is not interested at all in the differences between the various streams of that party. Once a Sicilian priest was shown the door when he tried to describe to him the weight of the Mafia in ecclesiastical affairs. I have the impression that he despises the Italian method of politics. He returned two days ago from the earthquake area in the south with his nerves in shreds. He said he was able to see the Government's indifference to the situation with his own eyes while going among the homeless. Even the newspaper of the Holy See pays less attention to Italian politics than in the past.'

'The Vatican Section of the KGB has always been an attentive reader of the *Osservatore Romano*. Each day I receive a summary of all the most important articles it prints.'

'Two years have already passed since Wojtyla's election,' said the Monsignore, 'but the VIPs of the Italian clergy do not appear to be resigned to the presence of a Pope who will not condone their nefarious activities.'

'I remember your interesting report on the course of the last Conclave. The atheists are more dignified than the pious in disputing their high offices. In any case, they cannot protect their worldly ambitions by invoking the Holy Spirit.'

'Wojtyla would not have become Pope if the Italian cardinals had not been split into two factions. When the stalemate between Archbishop Siri of Genoa and Archbishop Benelli of Florence was seen to be insurmountable, it became necessary to consider a non-Italian candidate.'

'But why a Pole?'

'In the Vatican he has been named the Frontier Pope and the Pope who came in from the cold. The majority of the Conclave chose a man who was used to measuring himself against the other great universal church – Communism. From their point of view they are convinced they chose wisely, because only he who knows his enemy well has the best chance of being the victor.'

'We have crushed worse enemies then Wojtyla. Hitler pushed his Nazi mob even to the gates of Moscow, but we caught him like a rat in his Berlin bunker,' said Leonov.

'Stalin used Hitler when partitioning Poland. Brezhnev has to seek the help of a Pole to restore calm to Warsaw. History repeats itself with amusing variations,' laughed Comrade Monsignore, indicating a sign over a Tuscan *trattoria* along the Lungotevere Flaminio. 'We have arrived,' he said. 'Here we can have a delicious snack while continuing our conversation undisturbed.'

'Tomorrow morning we must submit an infallible plan to the Chief,' observed Leonov, and turning to his companion added: 'My head and your reputation as the Vatican Mole are at stake!'

Moscow

Although it had been proposed by Suslov and warmly received by Brezhnev, the manoeuvre of 'approaching the Pope' was agreed upon reluctantly by other members of the Politburo. The leading Communist Party of the world was secretly preparing to consult the Head of the Catholic Church – a living anti-Marxist symbol – inviting him to cooperate with the USSR in a peaceful solution to the Polish crisis.

If John Paul II rejected Moscow's initiative, and worse still if he denounced it to international public opinion, the Soviet Union would suffer the most serious humiliation in its history, even more painful than the withdrawal of its missiles from Cuba and Kennedy's threats to Khrushchev. This time the Leninist maxim whereby 'two steps forward and one step back' were sufficient to reach the winning post could be applied catastrophically, with the risk of taking too many steps backward in the struggle against the religious superstructures – 'opium of the people', according to Marxist teaching. But these general considerations did not take away the validity of Suslov's theory, which attributed to the Pope the ability to exercise a non-substitutable 'braking role' on the independent trade unions of Poland.

There were several reasons why it was necessary to act quickly in convincing the Pope to undertake the task of mediator. The internal Polish structure was aggravated by the approach of the first anniversary of the Soviet invasion of Afghanistan in December 1979. The Russian dissidents had circulated a bitter joke, according to which the entry of Soviet troops into Kabul would be celebrated by a solemn cortège of Red Army divisions marching through the streets and squares of Warsaw.

As Reagan was an unknown quantity, the Soviet leaders knew that it would be impossible to delay military intervention in Poland beyond 20 January 1981, but at the same time they were afraid of the political and psychological reactions of the non-allied countries of the Third World should the march on Warsaw take place excactly one year after the occupation of Afghanistan.

The vote made by the General Assembly of the United Nations some months before left no doubt of this. In the UN building the representatives of 104 countries subscribed to a resolution calling for the immediate withdrawal of all foreign troops from Afghan territory. Among the non-aligned countries, 56 supported the motion, 17 abstained, and only 9 rejected it in accordance with Moscow's wishes.

Brezhnev and his companions, much disappointed, had to acknowledge the attitude taken in the voting of the 49 African countries. Of these, 27 approved the resolution, 12 abstained, 7 did not use their vote, while 3 voted against. In the Islamic world condemnation of the Soviet invasion of Afghanistan was enormous, with the exception of two votes in favour of the Soviet position (that of South Yemen and the Afghan puppet regime presided over by Karmal), and four abstentions, of which Libya and Syria were quite understandable. With this at their shoulder, the Soviet leaders knew very well that an armed attack against Poland would unleash, if not exactly the third world war, at least a new wave of international hatred and disparagement of the militaristic and imperialistic politics of Moscow.

After having decided to knock at the doors of the Vatican to 'mobilize the Pope', Brezhnev and his collaborators would have to elaborate the undertaking, allowing them to arrive at their purpose quickly and with the maximum secrecy. The leaders of the Kremlin came to the conclusion that Brezhnev should personally assume the task of negotiating with the Pope to induce him to guarantee a *modus vivendi* between the Communist regime, the clergy, and the mass of Polish Catholics. To address John Paul II through diplomatic channels would have been possible but of no use. The Holy See does not have a Papal nuncio or an apostolic delegate in Moscow, and the Soviet Union has no ambassador in the

Vatican. A written message from Brezhnev to the Pope would have had to reach the Vatican State secretariat through the Russian Embassy in Rome, with the serious risk of its being intercepted before reaching its destination and, above all, the danger of its coming under the scrutiny of the Secretary of State, Cardinal Casaroli, and the Pope's private secretary, Monsignor Stanislaw Dzwisz.

Assuming that an emissary of the Soviet Embassy in Rome received authorization to deliver the message into the Pope's own hands, how could one be sure of an immediate answer? Before replying His Holiness would, presumably, want to consult Cardinal Wyszinsky and other members of the Polish episcopy. In this case the risk of a leak would be certain.

Gromyko delved into his small store of ancient Roman proverbs for a Latin admonition he had heard a long time ago during a meeting with the French Foreign Minister, Couve de Murville: *Verba volant scripta manent* ('Words fly, written words remain'). An element of prudence was advisable, whatever exchange of document took place between the Kremlin and the Vatican – the indomitable enemy of Marxist-Leninism. The Politburo could not trust the pontifical intermediaries, relayed and what had to be communicated to the Pope therefore had to be relayed by word of mouth. Khrushchev had understood this: he had used the services of his son-in-law Adjubei as a third party when speaking to the late Pope John XXIII.

Gromyko's objections were valid. Now it was necessary to decide who was going to undertake the mission to the Pope in the name of Brezhnev. The Prime Minister, Nikolai Tikhonov, who had recently taken over from the sick Kosygin, declared himself ready to go incognito to Rome – alone or with Gromyko – to confer with John Paul II. 'Fortunately, my face is almost unknown in the West so no one will be aware of my presence in Italy,' he said to his companions, who listened to him with understandable surprise. 'If the Pope agreed, I could go to him tomorrow as the meeting would be conducted without any form of publicity. The KGB can certainly find the means to take me to the Vatican without exciting any curiosity or gossip.'

The head of the Soviet secret service, Yuri Andropov, was called, and he gave the assurance that there was no problem in slipping a Russian tourist through the bronze portals of the Vatican City, though the physical protection of Prime Minister Tikhonov might be difficult to ensure during a clandestine visit to a non-socialist country.

'Our Government cannot ask the Vatican to grant either a private or an official audience, and we cannot endanger Tikhonov's safety,' observed Brezhnev, interrupting the debate. 'At the same time we must prevent the Pope from directing us towards his Secretary of State or other cardinals: we have to speak to him and to him alone. The Polish situation has been exacerbated from the time Wojtyla went to sit on that so-called "Chair of Peter". That is why his cooperation has become indispensable in easing the crisis. I think the only way to make him understand the reality of the situation is for a face-to-face discussion between him and me. Naturally, I am not disposed to go to the Vatican, and as we understand that the Pope cannot come to Moscow, we must persuade him to agree to a meeting with the utmost urgency in a place convenient to us both.'

'But is it possible to find a "place of common convenience" for an encounter between the Pope and the President of the USSR?' This question, with its multiple aspects, was uppermost in the minds of all members of the Politburo.

It was decided that the meeting would not take place on Vatican soil or in any place sacred to the Catholic Church. It would be a condition that whatever place was chosen the two interlocutors must be able to converse freely and remain completely undisturbed by any third party.

The task of planning a meeting acceptable both to Brezhnev and to the Pope was entrusted to Yuri Andropov who, as head of the KGB, was not short on inventiveness. He was to submit his plan to Brezhnev and would be responsible for all aspects of organizing the operation. Andropov had a week to prepare for this meeting, which was to take place at the earliest time possible. A trip to Rome was essential so that he could study the movements and habits of the Pope.

The suggestion that John Paul II could be kidnapped and taken to Brezhnev was certainly not to be considered, as the President of the USSR desired to solicit Papal cooperation in a relaxed atmosphere and not through force. Force could be applied later, against Poland, if Karol Wojtyla was deaf to Brezhnev's pleas.

Rome

Yuri Andropov, head of the KGB, crouched over the maps of the Vatican City and the Papal residence of Castel Gandolfo, and carefully studied the alternative plans detailed by Sergei Leonov – with the assistance of 'Comrade Monsignore' – for the secret meeting between Brezhnev and the Pope.

'You're right, Sergei,' said Andropov after a long silence, turning to Leonov who was seated on the other side of the desk. 'We have to descend from the sky. We will select one plan or the other according to the time chosen by Moscow.'

The 44 hectares of the Holy See were contained and detailed on the sheet of paper under their eyes. 'At this moment,' observed Leonov, pointing to St Peter's Square, 'the crowds are beginning to gather from every quarter to hear the Pope's midday sermon. If you like, comrade, we can turn on the television and make the sign of the cross.' He laughed nervously, oppressed by the tension which had contributed towards a sleepless night.

The map clearly showed Bernini's colonnade enclosing the square, and the obelisk erected in front of the main doors of the Basilica. An arrow indicated the balcony from where the Pope gives his blessing, *Urbi et Orbi*. On one side of the Basilica the 'Holy Door' was visible, opened every quarter of a century in celebration of Holy Year. 'We certainly have to praise the Vatican architects for building the Pope's city so rationally: a third of it buildings; a third streets, squares and courtyards; a third gardens. I propose that the Kremlin is rebuilt along the same lines.' This time it was Andropov who laughed at his own words.

'Which holds the most treasures, St Peter's or the Hermitage in Leningrad?' Leonov enquired idly.

They were ensconsed in an office of the Soviet Embassy in Rome, in the Via Gaeta. The arrangements for the 'Andropov Mission' in the Italian capital had been entrusted to a local agent of the KGB, Natasha Ranskolnieva, who had been at the Embassy in Rome for the past three years as a secretary. Natasha was an old acquaintance of agent Sergei Leonov. They had worked together once before, when she was at the beginning of her activity abroad at the Soviet Embassy in Athens, and he had been sent to Greece at the time of the colonels to make contact with the opposing Communists. Ukrainian by origin, Natasha was just over thirty and unmarried. She had the look of a lady brought up in a peasant environment; thick chestnut hair framed a radiant and lively face, rosy cheeked and free of make-up. Swelling and provocative breasts distracted masculine admiration from her muscular thighs. The legs were long and straight with rounded calves that could, if necessary, withstand a long, hard march.

Natasha was on her first assignment abroad for the KGB when they met. Sergei, ten years older, was already a trusted official in the secret service and clearly destined for a splendid career. They took an immediate liking to each other. Although married with two children, Sergei found (or believed he had found) in her the embodiment of Soviet patriotism. She was born into a rural family, brought up close to the bosom of great Mother Russia; wanting to improve herself socially she attended technical school and qualified in mechanical engineering. When very young she was recruited into the KGB for her knowledge of radio communications, and was trained in receiving and transmitting secret messages, planting bugging devices, intercepting, and decoding. In Natasha's eyes Sergei symbolized success, and had already aroused the admiration and approval of his superiors for his achievements. He brought her, as she loved to repeat, the 'smell of home', reminding her of boundless fields, of the steppes and the great rivers, and seemed to carry the cupolas of Red Square reflected in the depths of his grey eyes.

In their spare time she took him to the Parthenon, to the birthplace of the Olympic Games, and to the taverns flowing with resinous wines. The admiration that she felt for her more experienced colleague – who taught her many things, and who was considered to be one of the most able exponents of the middle generation – rapidly grew to a feeling of affection. Although scrupulously following the security regulations forbidding any indiscretion with regard to past assignments, she believed that he had participated in missions of the utmost importance. She was fascinated by his allusory tales, which perhaps made her imagine more than was absolutely true. He reciprocated her interest with a kind of condescension fed by the curiosity to know her more intimately. Both were aware of the disciplinary risks they would face in breaking the KGB's internal code of conduct if they became lovers.

A favourable occasion for a brief affair arose when they went on leave to the Peloponnese and spent an unforgettable few hours on the romantic island of Hydra.

They lost touch after that, not knowing if they would ever meet again. She was transferred to Ottawa, where she remained for four years, then to Rome. He was kept for a while in Moscow, in his sea of dossiers at Central Operations, where he became one of the most trustworthy collaborators of the head of the KGB – Andropov.

It was Natasha who had to book the hotel room for Sergei Leonov. When she was told there were no single rooms available and that the guest would be put in a double room, she thought she saw a sign of destiny.

They met in the livid light of dawn, as soon as Leonov had parted from 'Comrade Monsignore', and wandered through the streets of the city centre, among drunks, beggars, prostitutes and police vans, happy that they had met again. Finally they found themselves at the Trevi fountain – that place of ritual pilgrimage. The boys jumping into the water to collect the coins would later fish out Leonov's kopeks also. At his hotel in the early hours of the morning Natasha and Sergei went to bed, to lie, for a short while, warm and close together. Then they hurried to the Embassy, but not at the same time, hoping that no one had discovered their slight infringement of regulations.

Yuri Andropov, the inaccessible 'Chief', had always been a

legendary figure to Natasha, but now unforeseen circumstances (the details of which had been kept from her by Sergei) allowed her to see him at close hand.

Before Andropov and Leonov shut themselves in the office placed at their disposal by the Embassy, Natasha had to carry out a routine inspection to make sure that the walls and fixtures were 'clean' – that is, free from any listening device planted by an outside source. The inspection was thorough and the room was pronounced safe. With a feminine touch she then served coffee before leaving them to their discussion. As she was about to leave the room, Andropov, his voice harsh, asked: 'Are you free tonight, Comrade Ranskolnieva?'

Her cheeks aflame with surprise and embarrassment, she replied that she was. In a peremptory manner, more a command than an invitation, Andropov added: 'I trust you would like to show me the attractions of Roman nightlife?' Sergei remained rigid on his chair without batting an eyelid. A good agent, of the KGB or any other secret service, learns quickly to keep cool in any circumstances. Agent Sergei now had to prove to himself that he was master of his feelings, while his girlfriend was snatched from under his nose in the name of that universal law whereby the strongest flourish even under the egalitarian system that the Communist regime proclaims to be.

The brief, erotic interlude confirmed that what he felt for Natasha was mainly physical, and therefore he could not claim any hold on her. He presumed that Andropov did not know of the situation between him and Natasha, though perhaps he sensed something and had decided to put an obstacle in their path so as not to have to mete out harsh discipline.

Sergei was asking himself this when he was sharply brought back to the present by Andropov saying: 'One of our SS20 warheads would be enough to destroy all of this, plus what the priests call pagan Rome, entirely.' He placed the palm of his hand on the map of the Vatican. 'The Pope can count himself lucky in that we want to negotiate with him after he put the Polish timebomb between our feet.'

Washington

On the morning of Monday 1 December 1980 a top secret message was transmitted in code by the Soviet Embassy in Washington to the Foreign Ministry in Moscow. The message was preceded by an official communiqué, also in code: 'For the attention of Foreign Minister Gromyko with the utmost possible urgency.' Ambassador Anatoly Dobrynin communicated that he had spent the weekend in California and added: 'Long conversation with "Cowboy". Awaiting urgent call on clean phone to give particulars.' Half an hour later the connection between Moscow and Washington was made. Shut in a special cabin in the Embassy protected from any outside interference, known in Soviet diplomatic jargon as the 'Talkie Den', Dobrynin imparted to his Chief the results of the meeting he had had with 'C' – always using the initial letter to indicate the unnamed person.

Gromyko encouraged him to give a detailed report. Its recording on tape would be heard later by the entire Politburo, who were anxious to know the outcome of the mission.

'According to the instructions received, I tried to psychoanalyse the subject of our interest. If I am allowed to begin with my conclusions, "C" gave me the impression of being a fanatic visionary from whom we can expect little good.'

'We knew that from the beginning,' interrupted Gromyko. 'It is the same individual who talked about anti-Communist purges in the forties, when he was on the Board of the Screen Actors' Guild.'

'In his basic attitude he has not changed at all. We have to acknowledge the consistency of his bluntness. Fortunately, he has not inherited the religion of his father, who was a Catholic of Irish descent, but embraced the faith of his mother, a Scottish Protestant. He will cause us enough problems without being a puppet of the Vatican as well!'

'How did he receive you?' Gromyko enquired.

'I must say that as a host he was very kind. A point in his favour is that he prefers vodka to whisky; actually he never drinks whisky, which surprises and irritates many of his countrymen. He showed me around his ranch from end to end. I even had to climb up on one of his horses – called Gualianko.'

'I can't imagine you as a rancher,' laughed Gromyko.

'When he saw that horses were not my forte, he drove me in his jeep to see the most beautiful parts of his ranch. It extends to about 280 hectares and has a spectacular view of the Pacific Ocean from an altitude of more than 600 metres. Afterwards, we sat by the fire and discussed affairs for three hours.'

'Tell me what you ascertained, beginning with Poland.'

'"C" reserves the right to retaliate should we decide to move in.'

'What kind of retaliation?'

'He didn't tell me. But he quoted a phrase of his Secretary of State, General Haig, saying that he was ready to subscribe to it: "There are more important things than peace. There are things which we Americans must be willing to fight for."'

'Is Poland one of those things?' demanded Gromyko anxiously.

'On this question his reply was not explicit, but he said that the Soviet Union must be convinced that the results of an invasion of Poland would be very severe. He repeated that the United States under his leadership would not be "kicked around by anybody". He frequently uses the imagery of Western films and always speaks as though he were waiting for the applause of his fans.'

'Did he mention any other form of reprisal, apart from war?'

'He said that he would answer force with force. It would be one of the many possibilities at his disposal. He wants the leaders of the Kremlin to prepare themselves for strong reaction – for example, a quarantine with regard to world trade or even a blockade of Cuba. He is convinced that the Soviet can only understand "tooth for a tooth" tactics. He has stated that we will get no concessions from him unless there are concessions in return. He underlined many times that the Soviet Union is not yet self-sufficient almost seventy years after the October revolution. I got the impression that he would not hesitate to starve us if he could.'

'But what about the so-called blockade of Cuba? We must inform Castro immediately,' said Gromyko.

'His point is that Cuba has become a Soviet colony, 145 kilometres off the coast of America. If we were to attack Poland he would consider himself at liberty to strangle Cuba in order to punish our affront. That would be one way to reply without going all out towards a third world war.'

'Besides Poland, is he willing to make any new agreement on disarmament?'

'He boasts that he is willing to negotiate an arms limitation treaty with us, but repeats that he will not stand by the SALT agreement, which – in his opinion – has given the Soviet Union the advantage of 3000 more nuclear warheads. He wants the negotiators to go back to the table and come up with what he calls a fair and genuine agreement for strategic nuclear weapons.'

'Did he give you any sermon on human rights?'

'Of course. He stated that there are no human rights in the Soviet Union, as there are none under Castro. According to his informants, the Cubans enjoyed more human rights under Batista than under Castro. For this reason he will be inclined to grant protection to the governments of small countries that in some instances, faced with internal dissent, violate human rights. He mentioned South Korea as an example. In other words: better to feed a dictatorship friendly towards the United States than to give way to a pro-Communist regime.'

'What else did you get from the talk?'

'I was able to admire his collection of riding boots and the colourful gaucho hats hanging on the walls of the ranch. I consider them as the symbols of his childish politics. "C" seems to be ready to march against imaginary enemies at any time. His belligerent way of speaking also applies to his fellow Americans. He calls them "the heroes", as if they were born to fight. I warned you that he is a dreamer. How else can you describe a man who proclaims that he can see heroes every day going in and out of factory gates, and even heroes across the counter in the supermarkets? The people who elected him describe this way of thinking as patriotism. I would rather say that the man is crazy. Let us not forget that his father was an alcoholic, although only periodically – as he explains. In his family they considered the alcoholism of the father as a sickness: certainly a mild way to put it!'

'You have given us a clear picture, Anatoly. We can assume that he is a dangerous dreamer.'

'He will tell you that the American soldiers went to Vietnam for a "noble cause" and that they lost the war only because Washington, at that time, was "afraid to win". He admits that the first task of a statesman is to preserve the peace, but is very quick to add: "It must not be peace at any price; it must not be a peace of humiliation and gradual surrender."'

'Surrender to whom?' asked Gromyko.

'To the Soviet Union, naturally. Carter used to say that the United States are "second to none". He has modified that slogan by recognizing that they have already become "second to one": which means, to us.'

'Should we provide him with tranquillizers?' suggested Gromyko.

'At the moment I see no chance of bringing him back to reality. How can you impart good sense to a man who says: "We are too great a nation to limit ourselves to small dreams"? He likes to dream big! And finally: what good can we expect from a man who calls his wife "mummy", while she feeds him jelly beans?'

Moscow

After having examined the report sent by Ambassador Dobrynin confirming Reagan's intransigence, the Politburo immediately called for a summit conference of the Warsaw Pact countries to discuss the developments in the Polish crisis.

The delegations invited by the 'brother countries' were presided over by Nicolai Ceausescu of Romania, Gustav Husak of Czechoslovakia, Erich Honecker for the German Democratic Republic, Todor Zhivkov of Bulgaria, Janos Kadar of Hungary, and Stanislaw Kania, the successor to Gierek at the helm of the Polish Communist Party, flanked by the Prime Minister Jozef Pinkowski and by the Foreign Minister, the Defence Minister and the Minister of the Interior.

The heads of the delegations took their places around a huge table in the conference hall of the Kremlin, after having been greeted warmly by Leonid Brezhnev, some being honoured by a kiss on the mouth according to the custom of the Soviet hierarchy when meeting foreign comrades deserving affectionate treatment.

Brezhnev was surrounded by the 'Four Horsemen of the Apocalypse', who had together planned with him the secret meeting with the Pope in a last attempt to avoid the invasion of Poland: the Prime Minister, Nikolai Tikhonov, the Foreign Minister, Andrei Gromyko, the Minister of Defence, Dmitri Ustinov, and the head of the KGB, Yuri Andropov.

In front of each delegate seated at the table was a leather folder containing writing paper, pens and pencils; bottles of mineral water and non-alcoholic drinks, glasses, metal boxes of cigarettes of the various countries represented, and ashtrays. At the end of the hall, in plywood-panelled cabins, sat the interpreters, while earphones were at the disposal of each delegate.

With short intervals for working lunches and dinners, the sitting went on for two days.

The meeting which took place in the afternoon of Friday 5 December 1980 was restricted to delegation heads and lasted two and a half hours; during that time the other members and interpreters withdrew to an adjoining chamber to continue their own discussions.

When the delegations reconvened in a plenary sitting Brezhnev read out a final communiqué which was to be circulated to the Press.

The document, approved unanimously, was worded in very vague terms on the real intention of the Socialist Alliance with regard to the Polish crisis. This document assured Poland that 'she could count on the solidarity and fraternal help of her allies', and at the same time expressed the conviction that the Polish government would be able to resolve the country's internal problems alone.

Reading between the lines, the communiqué did not exclude the possibility of military intervention in the future, even if conceived as a proof of solidarity and fraternal help, should the Polish authorities be unable to 'normalize' the solution according to the schemes dictated by Moscow.

As foreseen, Stanislaw Kania, the new head of the Polish Communist Party, found himself at the centre of the cyclone during the debate held behind closed doors. In his capacity as chairman of the conference, Brezhnev invited those present to allow Kania to submit his preliminary report without interruption. At the end of his speech they would be free to formulate questions or objections.

Kania began, his voice trembling slightly with emotion, in contrast to his stocky thick-set bulldog body, poised to spring. Slowly, as he continued, his voice acquired confidence, perhaps because of the benevolent glances from under bushy eyebrows that Brezhnev cast towards him from the other side of the table.

The Polish leader said that he felt the need to explain to his comrades of the USSR and other 'brother countries' the phenomenon of the rapid growth of independent trade unions grouped under the name of Solidarity, which had already

36

reached 10 million members, while the Polish Communists remained in the region of 3 million, of whom 250,000 were officials and fulltime employees of the Party sections. In analysing the reasons for this disparity Kania admitted that the visit of the Pope to Poland between 2 and 10 June the previous year had had a catalytic and explosive effect on the mass of practising Catholics. For the first time they had become aware of their force as well as their discipline and organizational capacity.

'Comrades,' said Kania, looking around and waving his arms, 'only he who has been a witness can understand what that visit meant to the life of my country. If the Pope had preached civil war he would have won without encountering any resistance. Comrades, we must not forget that Karol Wojtyla is a son of the people. It is not astonishing that the Poles, seeing him return dressed in white, filled the streets and squares to acclaim him. The same intoxicated scenes took place in Ireland, the United States, France, Brazil, the African countries, and even in Turkey, where the Catholics are ony a small minority. If, before the Pope's visit, the Polish dissidents could have been compared to a small, easily controllable fire,' explained Kania, 'after his departure that fire assumed devouring proportions, threatening the very roof and foundations of the socialist state.'

Despite this, Kania was optimistic about the recovery of the Government and the Polish United Workers' Party. The mistakes of the Gierek administration, which had spread the discontent even to the Communist cadres, had already been partly corrected. Economic aid from the most prosperous of socialist countries would allow them to be removed completely, on the understanding that the new Polish administration and its foreign allies kept their blood cool and were not overcome by panic.

Kania admitted that malignant growths had appeared on the organ tissues of the Polish nation. More than forty trade unions were already adherent to the Solidarity movement, among them the chimneysweeps and gardeners. A dispute was brought before the Supreme Court after the small farmers had asked to be allowed to constitute their own independent union. This request caused special problems as its granting would endanger agricultural productivity.

'We cannot permit the luxury of playing about with independent trade unions in the food sectors while the population complain of the long queues outside the butchers' shops. We are trying to make the small farmers and the labourers who support them understand this.'

'To fight this malignancy,' continued Kania, returning to his comparison of the situation with a sick body, 'you have two methods of treatment: to cut out the growth or to treat it with a bombardment of high energy ions. If we do use the scalpel, no one can be sure of the complete removal of the growth. My opinion, and that of my comrades of the Warsaw Central Committee in whose name I speak, is that we should have the scalpel ready but without using it, in the hope that we can weaken the malignancy with gamma-rays so that it ceases to reproduce – we do not want it eradicated from one place to appear in another. We have placed ourselves on this course of action with the independent trade union Solidarity, subscribing to the Agreement of Gdansk of 31 August.'

Kania specified that the flexibility of the Communist Party and the Polish Government would have definite and insurmountable limits. 'We are, for example, inflexible in rejecting the demands for a public trial against Gierek and his comrades who have been removed from their posts. No one dreams of returning to the system of justice of the pre-Gomulka era. Undoubtedly Gierek and the others will have to account to the Party for their actions. They have already paid in part with their dismissal. We cannot throw them as food for wild beasts, because beasts get excited at the smell of human blood.'

The Polish leader's report dwelt briefly on the criteria of the internal purification the Party had undergone in punishing the mistakes committed during the time of Gierek. This purification was severe, but should not turn into an uncontrollable witch-hunt. The assignment of duties and offices under the direct leadership of the Party had been drastically and minutely reviewed. The promised reform of the governing apparatus would be completed against the resistance of bureaucracy.

Kania insisted on the necessity of intensifying State control on Church affairs, taking advantage of the formula of 'democratizing the religious cult'. At the end he said that his country was on the threshold of a very hard winter. Shortages of food and energy supplies increased the people's impatience, offering new bait to those who wanted to fish in troubled waters. This is why Poland had more than ever to trust in the cohesion and mutual assistance of the family of socialist countries.

Rome

Natasha dressed herself with extra care on the evening that she had to accompany Yuri Andropov on his tour of Rome, choosing a soft pink cashmere dress under a fur jacket, and high-heeled boots. She wanted very much to impress the Chief, not only for the furtherance of her career but also in the hope that his influence could help her in the aims and desires she nurtured for Sergei. If Andropov had been on their side, their liaison might have progressed more rapidly, perhaps with an opportunity arising for both of them to be assigned to the same post. The transfer of personnel from one city to another was decided by the KGB head himself, according to international needs.

She informed Andropov's bodyguards of the proposed itinerary. According to the Chief's instructions, vigilance must be carried out at a discreet distance so as not to spoil his enjoyment of the evening.

A car was put at his disposal and Natasha sat at the wheel, driving with confidence through the chaotic maze of streets and hair-raising traffic. Their first stop was at the Capitol, its statues, temples and arches floodlit, and then to the darkness of the tree-covered Palatine Hill, wrapped in an eerie silence. Many centuries ago, here in this little space, the destiny of the civilized world had been decided. A short distance from the ruins of the Forum was the imposing white bulk of the monument to Victor Emmanuel II and the Tomb of the Unknown Warrior. Nearby stood the Palazzo Venezia, with the famous balcony from where the Fascist dictator Benito Mussolini harangued the crowds, and the announcement of Italy's entry into the Second World War had been made. As they crossed the Via del Corso, Andropov asked her to pull up in front of a shop selling menswear; he carefully noted the prices of the goods on display in the window.

'Before I leave,' he said, returning to the car, 'I shall buy a tie for each member of the Politburo – my comrades appreciate Roman fashion very much. Did you know that Comrade Khrushchev had a suit made for him every year by Angelo Litrico? How he would strut up and down, preening himself . . . who knows where Litrico's model of Khrushchev's measurements are now, I wonder. Should you find out, Comrade Natasha, you must let me know.' They continued on their way towards the Colosseum, which the Romans describe as a slice of gruyère cheese because of the rows of arches piercing its length throughout. 'This is where the Roman emperors sacrificed their slaves, feeding them to the lions,' explained Natasha.

'I wonder what treatment is reserved for the slaves of today?' mused Andropov. 'I have seen many beggars on the streets.'

'Don't be taken in by appearances. Many of them sleep on mattresses stuffed with banknotes, while those suffering genuine hardship do their best to hide it.'

'I want to meet the genuine poor – those who have to struggle to survive under exhausting conditions.'

'Even the concept of hard work has a different meaning in Italy,' replied Natasha. 'Here there are those who pretend to work and do nothing, and those who kill themselves to make ends meet while keeping a smile on their lips. But we will go and see some typical examples of the Roman proletariat in the Trastevere district.' Before taking Andropov to the old, picturesque quarter of the Trastevere, Natasha wanted to show him as many interesting sights as she could in the time at their disposal. Down the Via dei Trionfi they went, between the Palatine and the Aracaeli, skirting the Circus Maximus, before reaching the tree-lined avenue running alongside the Baths of Caracalla, weaving in and out of the traffic. Going through St Sebastian's Gate they came to the start of the Appian Way – the ancient road that runs south, finally to reach the port of Brindisi on the heel of Italy. The cobbled way is lined with ruined villas, mausoleums, aqueducts, set against the backdrop of the Alban hills, with dark cypresses and ilex, and interspersed with the modern villas of wealthy industrialists and film stars.

Andropov, sitting next to Natasha, murmured over and over again: 'Beautiful, really beautiful,' and in his enthusiasm placed his hand on her thigh, possessively. Natasha continued to point out the surrounding landmarks as though she was unaware of his hand pressing into her thigh through the wool dress, but pleased that the Chief had shown his admiration not only of the Roman views but also of her. When they reached the centre of the Trastevere Andropov said that he wanted to speak to the street vendors of roast meats, nuts and sweets. With Natasha acting as interpreter, he asked them what their daily wage was and about their family life; the number of children they had, what kind of education was provided, health insurance – all the time making notes in a little book he carried. 'A comparative study between conditions of the proletariat here in Rome and in Moscow is impossible as many of their occupations do not exist in our country. I notice that the vendors are able to carry on their trade in the open in the middle of winter.'

'Snow hardly ever falls here,' explained Natasha. 'I have only seen it fall once in the last three years.'

They went to the fashionable and always crowded Meo Patacca restaurant for supper, where the folk singers wandered among the tables dedicating songs to the clients. Natasha ordered the food but Andropov selected the wine, choosing a Corvo di Salaparuta – one bottle of red and one of white.

'I have heard,' he said, with the confidence of a connoisseur, 'that this is one of the best Sicilian wines.' At the end of the excellent meal he suggested that they should go somewhere quiet for a drink. Natasha agreed and they drove to the Tre Scalini in the Piazza Navona. A very mellow Andropov sat back in the warm luxury of the bar and sipped his cognac, looking with unconcealed admiration at Natasha. 'You are one of the most valuable assets of the Rome bureau,' he said, the smile accompanying the words explicit in its meaning. He had another brandy, gulped it down quickly and suggested that she drove him back to the residence for a little chat and to explain to her the reason for his appearance in Rome. Natasha accepted the invitation, preparing herself for a long night.

42

Moscow

The debate opened by Brezhnev on Kania's report rapidly assumed bitter tones. The Polish leader became the object of polemical comments and severe reproof, which were in large part directed not against him personally but against the collective administration, past and present, of the Warsaw Communist Party.

The Agreement of Gdansk was ruthlessly criticized by the German, Honecker, because in his opinion it constituted 'the unconditional surrender of the Polish Government and an inadmissible subversive plot of Western capitalism'. Pointing an accusatory finger at the entire Polish delegation, Honecker declared that a frightening abyss had been opened behind the back of the German Democratic Republic. 'My country does not intend to fight indefinitely on two deteriorating fronts. Our vigilance has up to now been directed against the plots of revanchism that emanate from Bonn. The new situation constrains us to fear traps even from Poland. We know that many members of Solidarity are also members of the Polish United Workers' Party. But Comrade Kania has not explained to us how this ambivalence can be allowed. Should the crisis be aggravated and develop into open conflict between the two institutions, would these self-styled Communists of Solidarity offer their loyalties to the Party or to the union?'

The Czechoslovak, Husak, intervened in the discussion to point out that the dangers exemplified by Honecker were made even more serious by the relative strengths of the Communist Party and Solidarity. The concession of autonomy to the independent trade unions had created a new centre of power with foreseeable and unpropitious effects on the solidity of the socialist state. 'We had to work hard to come out of the so-called "Prague Spring" undamaged, and we do not want to see our Polish comrades emerging from the "Summer of Gdansk" with broken bones.'

Brezhnev, who had listened in silence until now, chilled his listeners by commenting: 'Comrade Kania has referred to things that confirm our preoccupation. Think what would happen if Solidarity, born as a union movement, one day wanted to be recognized as a political force.'

'In such an event, the regime of the Workers' Party would be crushed for ever,' declared the Bulgarian, Zhivkov.

Kadar, the Hungarian, took these words to exhort his comrades present not to become prey to an alarmist psychosis. 'We must try not to submit Poland to the purgatory experienced in Budapest in 1956. Fortunately, the Government in Warsaw is in the stable hands of comrades with clear ideas. Hungary would not have had to call upon the USSR for help, if power had not been in the weak hands of Nagy, whose mind was eaten up with illusions of a so-called social democratic mould.'

Kadar's thesis was immediately supported by the Romanian, Ceausescu: 'I ask you, comrades, to evaluate the undeniable crisis in Poland in its correct perspective. Is it really true that we are faced with the birth of a counter-revolutionary force? I would speak rather of a devolutionary trend pressing for economic reform.'

Brezhnev thumped his fist on the table. 'Comrade Ceausescu is showing an ingenuousness which, if we didn't know him so well, could be suspected as treachery. The transformations called for by the self-styled Warsaw reformists would radically transform the economic structure making Poland irreconcilable as a socialist state.'

'Well said,' replied Honecker. 'We all know what happened in Yugoslavia. Belgrade also started to speak of a devolutionary policy by offering the workers a new model for self-management. To achieve this result Marshal Tito went to plot with Washington. Now Tito is dead, but I do not see one of his successors here at our side. Poland cannot and must not become a new Yugoslavia. The German Democratic Republic is ready to prevent this happening – even if it has to fight alone.' Brezhnev nodded in agreement, underlining Honecker's words.

'The historical circumstances, together with the geographical situation of Yugoslavia, prevented Stalin from impeding Tito's defection. But a repetition of that mistake in Poland would signify the suicide of the Socialist Alliance. Tito had economic difficulties to use as an alibi for turning to Washington for protection. We understand the real difficulties in Poland and we are giving copious transfusions of blood to get her on her feet, but we will not permit the sacrifices of the socialist family to be squandered in senseless reforms as set down in the Agreement of Gdansk!'

The President of the USSR took a paper from the folder in front of him and held it up in the air. 'Here is the Agreement of Gdansk set out in twenty-one points. I will comment briefly on them.

'First point. "Free trade unions based on Convention 87 of the International Labour Organization, as recognized in Poland." We have already discussed this and I think there is little to be added. The idea of a free trade union is repellent because it contradicts the principles of the Socialist state. The workers of the capitalist countries have the complete right to appeal for freedom against the dictates of the bosses. But what sense would freedom have for the workers against the hegemony of the proletariat, in the socialist countries? It is like standing in front of a mirror fighting with oneself.

'Second point. "The guaranteed right to strike and non-victimization of strikers and their helpers." Absolute nonsense – for the same reasons as before!

'Thirdly. "Freedom of speech and of the Press, a ban on prosecution of independent publishers, and access to the mass media for all religious denominations." Fortunately, on this point a form of censure was agreed for protection of State, economic and military security, although it was added that such decisions will be open to challenge in the courts.

'Four. "Reinstatement of those dismissed after the strikes of 1970 and 1976, and that students dismissed from university for their political views be allowed to resume studies." In other words, freedom for some of those snakes who are now in gaol.

'Five. "An announcement on the official media of the creation of a strike committee and its demands." Ridiculous!

'Six. "Action to lead the country out of the present crisis by publication of full information on its economic and social situation, by enabling all groups in society to participate in discussions on a national reform programme." Do we have to associate with the chiefs of Wall Street and the City of London in these discussions?

'Seven. "On strike pay. The Government agrees to payments for the strike period." These Polish strikers are very generous. They only ask for pay when they could also ask to be conferred with a medal for dereliction of duty!

'Eight. "Increase in wages by at least 14 zloty a month for the lowest paid and 500 zloty for the highest paid." Here it is difficult to understand if the union bigheads want to revitalize the national economy or bankrupt it.

'Nine. "Pay to be automatically adjusted to inflation." Showing a sudden glimmer of wisdom, the Gdansk negotiators have postponed a decision on this point.

'Ten. "Maintenance of full food supplies and the export of surpluses only." As I have already told my Polish comrades, the Soviet Union will intensify the export of foodstuffs into Poland. With a full belly even the unionists of Warsaw should be able to reason better.

'Eleven. "A ban on commercial prices for meat and the sale of home produce for hard currency." This is good and will bring about the abolition of a two-tier meat pricing system with higher prices paid for better cuts, replacing it with a single compromise price.

'Twelve. "Abolition of favouritism in promotion for Party members, and an end to special privileges for police and security services." Comrade Kania is an example of favouritism in promotion, as he was called upon as a substitute for Edward Gierek. Who will decide the merits for the next promotions within the Communist Party? I hope that at least this will remain entrusted to our Communist comrades and not be given to Solidarity administrators.

'Thirteen. "Meat to remain rationed until the market situation improves." This is a painful necessity which we will try to overcome as soon as possible.

'Fourteen. "Reduction in the retirement age to 55 for men and 50 for women, or after 30 and 25 years of work respectively." I see that the Polish trade unionists have little faith in the stamina of the workers. If this agreement was applied to the letter, the approval of which has been prudently postponed, none of us would be sitting here today around this table.

'Fifteen. "Improvements in pensions." Why not? The importance is to have the money available.

'I'll spare you the reading of the remaining points regarding old age and child allowances, reduction in the waiting time for new homes, and the increase of the daily allowance for official trips. These are technicalities on which our Polish comrades know how to make the appropriate decisions. But I will call to your attention the twenty-first point, which asks for more free Saturdays. Once again the trade unionists of Solidarity have shown that they have no clear idea of reality. According to our calculations Polish exports must increase by 30 per cent a year if the Warsaw Government wants to honour its debts, which fall due in the next three years, on schedule. Comrade Kania, with whom I spoke separately before this meeting, told me that the State's present debt burden is approaching ten billion dollars a year. There is no doubt that Poland is by far the most heavily indebted country of our Alliance. And in these circumstances the Polish trade unions propose reducing working hours. This is pure folly, if not sabotage. How can we ask the workers of our countries to increase their output to help their Polish brothers, while these same Polish brothers fold their arms on a Saturday and strike from Monday to Friday? I would like to ask Comrade Janusz Obodowski, the Polish Labour Minister, about this but he is not with us today. I conclude, repeating that we must act with the maximum urgency if we do not want the Polish crisis to turn into an unstoppable canker.'

Brezhnev took a handkerchief from his pocket and wiped his perspiring forehead while comments of approval buzzed around him.

Rome

Andropov and Leonov had carefully studied the area where 'Operation Pilgrim' would be carried out. The undertaking had to be prepared to the last detail as there was no margin for error.

Yuri Andropov was not slow in convincing himself that a landing in the Vatican would have to be rejected, as the site of Rome's heliport is close to the encircling walls of the Holy See. Moreover, that heliport is very near to the great antennae and the offices of the Vatican radio and television station, and only a few metres from Giovanni's Tower – a good vantage-point for spectators coming to watch the arrivals and departures of the helicopters.

The heliport at Castel Gandolfo has the great advantage of being away from the urban centre of Rome. The guard of the Pope's country residence is reduced to the minimum necessary, both for logistic reasons and because the Pontiff goes to Castel Gandolfo mainly to rest or to meditate. A few of the Swiss Guards' rusting halberds are more than enough to protect His Holiness on his walks in the gardens or when swimming in the pool, which had been built for him after he jokingly said to the College of Cardinals: 'Better invest a few hundred thousand lire in installing a swimming pool to keep the Pope in good health, rather than millions for his funeral and a new Conclave!'

To ensure the success of the undertaking, at least two Soviet helicopters had to be at hand: one for the Very Important Person and the other for the escort – also to be utilized as a reserve in case of necessity. 'We have no wish to stay here with our faces in the dust like the American Marines who tried to free the hostages in Tehran,' said Andropov, passing to the examination of the operative phase.

A third helicopter had to be held ready for use in the centre of Rome as a precaution.

The USSR has no bases in Italy, and to fly at least three helicopters over Rome and its outskirts would have to obtain official permission from the Italian governing authorities. It would also be necessary to provide a valid reason for such a flight so as not to arouse suspicion.

The plan submitted by Sergei Leonov for approval by Andropov took into account both of these obstacles.

A few days before the head of the KGB arrived incognito in Rome, on the evening of 23 November a severe earthquake had devastated several regions in southern Italy. According to the news, unverified because of the many small villages still inaccessible to rescuers, digging was continuing; the dead and the missing (presumed to be buried under the rubble) numbered more than 4000, while the injured amounted to over 10,000. International support was promptly given to the population struck down in the disaster, by the consignment of medicines, tents, prefabricated houses, food, clothes, and other necessary items. The Federal Republic of Germany and Great Britain were the first to send in field hospitals, engineers, and firemen equipped and ready to help those districts devastated by the catastrophe.

The Soviet Union would ask to be associated with the consignment of aid by sending clothes, furs and blankets to Salerno, Avellino and Potenza – the towns most severely hit by the earthquake. These gifts would be put into the hands of the local Communist Party sections involved in distributing aid to the homeless. The items generously offered by the USSR would be loaded onto ships of the Soviet merchant navy and quickly sent to the Mediterranean. A squadron of Soviet helicopters, placed at the disposal of the International Red Cross, would be ready to transport this relief to its destination.

Moscow

At the meeting of 5 December 1980, which was confined to the heads of countries adherent to the Warsaw Pact, Brezhnev described 'Factor W' as a decisive element in the solution of the Polish crisis. By a strange play of circumstances the three persons who had become the 'standard bearers' in the dissent against the Communist regime all bore the initial W. Wojtyla in Rome, Wyszynski in Warsaw and Walesa in Gdansk were the apex of a triangle which Brezhnev called 'the trap of provocation'. Of the three, the electrician, 39-year-old Lech Walesa, who had headed the Gdansk strike, was the least dangerous because he acted as a puppet, following the commands of the other two.

'All this talk by the Western Press about Lech Walesa is aimed to distract public opinion from the puppet-masters who make him move: the Pope and the Cardinal,' explained Brezhnev. 'My comrades of the Soviet Politburo have reached the conclusion that it would be perfectly useless to shut Walesa's mouth, as it is perfectly useless to close the mouth of a ventriloquist's dummy. If Walesa is removed, another would immediately appear with a different name. The Catholic Church can produce these puppets one after the other without end. For this reason I have begged our Polish comrades, and I continue to do so, not to touch a hair of Lech Walesa's head, and to resign themselves to his presence. If the Polish crisis can still be resolved through negotiation, we must turn to the other initial Ws – Wojtyla and Wyszynski.

'For obvious reasons, Wyszynski can only guarantee a temporary truce. If the present Pope was not his friend and compatriot, he would already have had to relinquish the Primacy of Poland, because of his age and according to the decree of Pope Paul VI. No one was surprised when Wojtyla refused the resignation of Wyszynski, inviting him to stay in his post, as they are friends and accomplices of long standing.

51

We all know that it was Wyszynski who elected Wojtyla – first as Archbishop, then as Pope.

'We can speak to Wyszynski every day through the Polish comrades and through the ambassadors of our respective countries in Warsaw. But whatever Wyszynski pledges for "normalization" in Poland would have a short life and, therefore, would not bind the Pope, who will one day have to nominate a future Primate of Poland.

'These considerations have convinced us that we must approach the Pope and speak to him very clearly. Since the Catholic Church in Poland has snared these traps of provocation against the Soviet regime in Eastern Europe, it is up to the Church to remove them, otherwise the member countries of the Warsaw Pact will have no alternative but to spring the traps and re-establish order. In this way the biggest W will be faced with his responsibilities and will have to answer one way or the other. Before moving on to the description of our plan, we want to know if you are in agreement with the evaluation of the problem.'

The Romanian, Ceausescu, was the only one present to express any misgivings. He agreed with Brezhnev's theory that the Catholic Church had set snares, but it was just because of this that the countries of the Warsaw Pact should not take part in the instigator's games. Possible intervention in Poland, or even the threat of such intervention, would induce the West again to close ranks in the policy of 'rolling back' Communism, as stated by the American Secretary of State Dulles in the fifties. A new Iron Curtain would be raised in the centre of Europe and, consequently, the military alliance of NATO would be consolidated. The policy of détente, woven with difficulty over the past ten years, would fall to pieces, and the arms race would acquire a dizzy momentum, swallowing an even bigger slice of the economic resources of the Socialist countries. 'Is this what we really want?' demanded Ceausescu, with obvious dismay.

The question was taken up by Honecker. 'Not one of us is a warmonger, least of all a German who has lived through the tragedy of the Second World War. We are trying here to establish the limits of tolerance, beyond which the Socialist Alliance would have to defend itself with force. We recall that Marx defined Poland as "the thermometer of the intensity and vitality of all revolutions since 1798". To leave her in the power of counter-revolutionary forces would betray the Communist cause.'

The Bulgarian, Zhivkov, added: 'The new American President has already announced that he will call General Alexander Haig to be Secretary of State. This means that the foreign policy of the United States in the coming years will be controlled by the same man, who, until a few months ago, directed NATO's military maneouvres on our borders and installed thousands of missiles – pointing at our heads – in Western Europe. We cannot reply to Reagan's threats by deserting Poland. It would be the start of a headlong slide which would be overwhelming!'

Brezhnev took up the argument. 'Your comments confirm the conclusion reached by the Politburo. The Polish crisis has now reached a decisive phase: if the Catholic Church does not immediately give a sign of coming to its senses, we will have to resort to military intervention. I trust in your complete discretion in confiding to you that I am agreeable to having a personal meeting with the Pope, to put him to the test, and to explore his intentions in depth. I will tell him that the future of Poland depends on his attitude.'

A murmur of astonishment greeted the Soviet President's announcement. The Vaticanists had, some years before, witnessed the same reaction from the College of Cardinals when Pope John XXIII announced, for the first time, his intention of convening the Vatican Council, a decision which left an indelible mark in the history of the Church.

Brezhnev was aware that his words had caused amazement and great anxiety among his listeners, and wanted to reassure them. 'The talk between myself and the Pope will only take place if Wojtyla agrees to meet me secretly, before the end of the year, and outside the Vatican. We will send him a definite invitation in the next few days. I will not go into details because the plan is being studied by our secret service and is likely to be modified. However, I will personally inform you of developments. I just wanted to give you a slight hint to find out whether you supported me in this idea – no matter what its outcome.'

'This Pope will never accept a face-to-face encounter with the leader of the Soviet Union to discuss Polish affairs,' Zhivkov said, in a peremptory voice.

'It's worth trying,' suggested Ceausescu. 'Every effort is acceptable if it can avoid recourse to arms.'

'Even I approve of the idea,' said Husak, 'as only a direct confrontation can help us to understand where the Pope wants to go with this new policy of the Church, described by him as *transatio ad Slavos*. To move the epicentre of Catholicism towards the East could have beneficial effects on the peaceful coexistence of the people only if the Vatican recognized reality and did not persist in feeding the sentiments of hostility against Marxist doctrine. Not one of us has ever thought of opening a Communist cell in the Sistine Chapel.'

'I agree to the proposal for a direct confrontation with the Pope, but I must be reassured that this plan will not put Comrade Brezhnev at risk, who is again placing himself in the line of fire,' said Kadar.

'According to my humble point of view, a conversation with the Pope would only waste precious time without achieving any useful outcome,' Honecker blurted out. 'I commend the intentions which have inspired our Soviet comrades in this initiative, but I do not want our vigilance to be lessened. I ask Comrade Brezhnev, therefore, to describe the military alternative.'

Victor Kulikov, Marshal of the USSR, Commander-in-Chief of the Military Forces of the Warsaw Pact, was called to the conference hall; he went over to a large map of Eastern Europe which had been projected onto a portable screen. With a wooden pointer he indicated the distribution and displacement of the forces under his command. Kulikov was

54

in uniform, his chest covered with medals that jingled faintly as he pointed to the nerve centres mentioned in his explanation.

'As you know, the Red Forces have excellent bases in those allied countries particularly exposed to the danger of a frontal attack by the West,' he said, as a preamble. 'The German Democratic Republic has five divisions spread over five quarters – altogether more than 400,000 men and 7000 armoured vehicles, supported by the 7th Air Force, with at least 1000 planes, and in addition to this, two armoured divisions and four motorized divisions of the German Democratic Republic unified under the command of the Warsaw Pact which can be moved rapidly along the boundary lines of the Oder–Neisse. In the south-east of Poland – in the Carpathian region – the Soviet 8th Army waits with three armoured divisions, flanked by seven motorized divisions and squadrons of transport planes. Near the Baltic coast, between Kaliningrad and Brest, the military zones of Byelorussia and the Baltic can count on the 5th and 6th Armies, divided into ten armoured divisions, two motorized, and one air transport squad. The Baltic area is protected by the 11th Guard with four armoured divisions, six motorized, and one air transport squadron, to which is added an umbrella force of thirty fighters.'

This brief but impressive list detailed by Kulikov showed his audience a picture of Poland surrounded by about seventy armoured divisions able to mobilize within a few hours if such an order were given. The Soviet marshal added that the USSR had, on Polish soil, 26,000 men of the 20th and 38th armoured divisions plus a fighter force based at Legnica.

The Polish armed forces facing this powerful menace were made up of 200,000 men – of whom 150,000 were conscripts. Their equipment, recently modernized, comprised 30,000 armoured vehicles and 700 planes.

Obviously Kulikov's report could not anticipate the reaction of the Polish armed forces in the event of the other nations of the Warsaw Pact invading their country in the guise of 'brotherly aid'. The aggressors ought to expect resistance to the last drop of blood, as in the firing of the Warsaw ghetto during the Second World War.

Capri

On the hydrofoil that connects Naples with Capri in a half hour's crossing, Sergei and Natasha, their arms around each other's waists, looked as though they were embarking on a romantic interlude.

The small, fast vessel left the Mergellina quay emitting a strident blast of her siren, warning the fishing boats in the vicinity of her approach, and these immediately widened the gap to give the hydrofoil a clear path.

'See Naples and die,' said Sergei, quoting the old proverb. 'But I don't understand why one should die after seeing this city. I feel as though I want to live more intensely.' He squeezed Natasha's hand, and she huddled closer to him as a protection against the wind, which blew strongly. All the other passengers had gone below as it was cold and the sea was choppy. She indicated Castel Angioino, which had once been a royal residence, with its stark, crenellated towers reflected in the waters of the bay.

'They say that in that castle, in medieval times, a queen called Giovanna received her lovers by night and then killed them so that they would not divulge the secrets of the bedchamber.'

'Do you mean that she killed them with her own hands?'

'No. They left her at dawn with kisses and words of love, and as they went a trapdoor opened beneath their feet and they plunged down onto the rocks below. The cries for help from those who were not killed instantly were drowned by the noise of the waves beating upon the rocks.'

'Queens have often behaved as whores, but this Queen Giovanna was a murderess as well – a good reason for abolishing the monarchy entirely,' Sergei commented.

The hydrofoil sped across the surface of the water leaving a long trail of foam; now Vesuvius rose majestically before their eyes, overshadowing the bay and the city. 'It's such a pity the volcano doesn't smoke any more,' said Natasha. 'It seems like a sleeping giant – perhaps it will wake suddenly.'

The vessel sped past the islands of Procida and Ischia. Sergei carried binoculars with him, and these he focused on both, admiring the typical Mediterranean vegetation: vineyards, olive groves, citrus orchards. Procida was the smaller of the two islands lying between Ischia and Cape Miseno.

'I was at Casamicciola last June,' said Natasha. 'Ischia is famous for its thermal and mineral baths, and for the natural therapeutic mud. Did you know that? I could only stay for four days – unfortunately.'

'Were you alone?' asked Sergei, inquisitorially.

'What do you mean – alone? In Italy a woman, if she is not repellent, will not remain alone for very long. It all depends on the woman's selectivity in choosing her companions.'

'Have you had many admirers in Rome?' he insisted.

'You know we are very restricted in our movements. The Italian male has a possessive nature, not adaptable to our type of work. I have had to pretend to be married on more than one occasion to discourage particularly obstinate pesterers. Counsellor Murawiew had to escort me one entire week because a university professor of modern history would not leave me alone. He sent me flowers every morning.' She looked up at Sergei and smiled.

Another screech of the siren announced that the hydrofoil was about to enter the little harbour of Capri. Representatives from the hotels lined up on the quay, the names of their respective establishments emblazoned on their caps. 'Quisisana', 'Scalinatella', 'Gatto Bianco', 'La Pineta', 'La Certosella', and so on. One of the hotel porters went up to the couple as they disembarked and asked deferentially in English whether they required rooms. 'Thank you, no,' replied Natasha in Italian. They took the funicular railway up to the legendary Piazzetta where, now as then, all the well-known members of the international jet set have paused. The four bars in the Piazzetta still had tables and wicker chairs set out in

58

the open, which during the tourist season were occupied without interruption from dawn until far into the night.

'When Sartre came to Capri, he sat in that corner every evening with Simone de Beauvoir,' said Natasha, indicating a table outside the Bar Vuotto. 'They sipped drinks and discussed literature and politics.'

'We could do the same,' suggested Sergei, looking at the great clock on the campanile in the Piazzetta, 'and while away a couple of hours before our first link-up with Headquarters.'

They drank Campari soda while watching with interest the people strolling past them. The difference between the island population and visitors from the mainland was very pronounced; they differed widely in their way of dressing, in their gestures, and in their way of speaking. The Caprese woman, particularly the old, preferred to wear black or clothes in dark and sober hues, while the tourists – even those who dressed conservatively in their normal surroundings – abandoned their sobriety for an orgy of colour as soon as they disembarked from the ferryboats.

'I feel as though I'm taking part in an out-of-season carnival,' commented Sergei.

'The tourists want to forget their cares and problems and so try to change their skin,' observed Natasha, sipping her drink. A young woman crossed the Piazzetta wearing, twined in her hair, two waving pheasant feathers. 'The extravagances on Capri today are nothing in comparison with the times when the island was frequented by the old Roman nobility, by the Aga Khan, and by the emulators of Oscar Wilde. Prince Nanni would come to the piazza with his favourite parrot on his shoulder and discuss the events of the day. Countess Amalia dei Bergonzoli would display on her naked shoulders a sentence, written in lipstick, that read: "Don't ask me – just do it." The invitation could be interpreted any way you liked.'

Sergei listened with great interest. 'What do the islanders think of this strange fauna coming in from the sea?'

'They love them and at the same time hate them. They love them because they bring wealth to the island, and despise them because of their decadence. For years this island has been accustomed to receiving unbalanced people. It was the summer home of the Roman emperors and several streets still bear their names: Caesar Augustus, Tiberius . . .'

The clock in the piazza chimed the hour: it was eleven o'clock. 'To work,' said Sergei, rising.

'Which direction do we take?' he asked.

'It's a quarter of an hour's walk to the villa. Fortunately, motor vehicles are not allowed in the centre of Capri. If they were, as at Anacapri, the island would lose a great part of its magic.'

In Via Camerelle one of the street photographers who had become rich snapping visitors approached them, asking if they would like to have an instant photograph taken. Instinctively, Sergei covered his face with his hand, while Natasha, smiling, shook her head in refusal. The photographer was in no way surprised at such a reaction and continued along the street. There were many couples staying on Capri enjoying a brief affair who were anxious to remain unrecognized.

Slowly they strolled along the Via Tragara, glancing at the hotels, semi-deserted during the winter season. The open-air swimming pools were brim full of turgid water from the heavy and frequent rainfall, and from the leaves that had fallen from the overhanging trees. A few white-painted metal chairs, scattered at the sides of the pools, stood like unmoving ghosts.

They had to turn left before reaching Tragara Point, and climb the steep steps that led into the Via Tuoro. Now they were at one of the highest points of the island, overlooking the magnificent view of the Faraglioni – that great rocky promontory rising from the water as the natural sentinel of Capri.

'Are you happy that we are able to spend a few days together?' Natasha asked, anxiously. Sergei ran his hand through her thick, silky hair, pushing back a curl that had escaped its fastening. 'How could you possibly doubt it?'

'Some astral influence seems to draw us towards islands – first Hydra and now Capri . . . and tomorrow?'

60

'If Operation Pilgrim fails we will both find ourselves exiles on St Helena – following in Napoleon's footsteps.'

'I will follow you anywhere – now that I have found you again. Why did you never get in touch with me in all these years?'

'You know our limitations and restrictions – I don't have to explain. But why talk about it? Let's enjoy this spell of freedom. Whoever would have thought that we should be reunited with the blessing of Headquarters?' Sergei leaned towards her and lightly kissed her cheek.

They walked a few more yards, then Natasha stopped in front of the gate of an isolated villa through which could be seen a neglected garden. 'We have arrived,' she said.

Holding hands, and as though impatient to reach their love nest, they entered, the gate closing behind them on squeaking hinges, and went along the short path to the entrance of the villa. Natasha tapped with her knuckles on the door. After a little while a middle-aged woman appeared at the ground floor window. 'Who do you want?' she demanded in Italian, her voice guttural.

'Frau Ursula Riesman,' replied Natasha.

'Who sent you?'

'The Dilecta Estate Agency of Rome.'

'The rooms are ready. Wait a moment and I'll let you in.'

Two hours later a radio bridge was functioning between the villa in Capri and the cruiser *Kirov* – the pride of the USSR's navy – sailing in the Mediterranean.

Rome

The executive of the Italian Communist Party enthusiastically received the news that the Soviet Government had decided to send aid to the people of southern Italy struck by the earthquake of 23 November.

The Secretary General of the Party, Enrico Berlinguer, called the Communist leaders of the most stricken towns and villages to the Party headquarters to advise them personally of this important development.

'I have been informed by the Soviet Ambassador,' he said, 'that several vessels of the Russian merchant fleet are already on their way towards the Mediterranean with their holds loaded with clothes, blankets, shoes, tents, and other items of major necessity.'

Some trade unionists, as well as the Communist town councillors of Naples and other regions of the south, proposed that posters thanking the Soviet leaders for their generosity should immediately be affixed to the walls of buildings and in shop windows. A proof was prepared and approved of unanimously. It was a reminder that the Soviet Union had always been in the vanguard in the tests of brotherhood of the international proletariat.

Berlinguer added that the Soviet Embassy had asked the Italian Government for, and had obtained, special permission to use three Russian helicopters to transport the relief direct from the ships to the distribution centres.

'We know that many Western countries have already sent, and are continuing to send, every sort of aid for the earthquake victims. But you understand, comrades, that it should be a point of honour for us to praise highly the munificence shown by the USSR at this time.'

No one present doubted that the Italian citizens, blessed with this Soviet help, would vote for the Communist Party at the next local elections. 'As you know, the winter climate in

Russia is very hard,' observed one member, 'which means that the clothes and blankets of Russian wool will be the best that can be made to protect the human body from cold in sub-zero temperatures.'

Berlinguer read the text of a telegram he had sent to Brezhnev, in the following terms: 'Moved by the testimony of friendship shown by the Communist Party and by the Workers of the USSR, the people of southern Italy warmly thank you and beg that their sentiments are expressed to the Soviet comrades employed in the collection and transport of aid.'

The Secretary General of the Italian Communist Party said that the three Soviet helicopters would arrive in the Mediterranean on the aircraft carrier *Kiev*, sailing as an escort to the merchant convoy.

Loaded with gifts destined for the southern Italian population, the helicopters would be directed to Salerno, Avellino and Potenza – the three principal centres of the provinces devastated by the earthquake. In the meantime the Soviet merchant ships would anchor in the port of Naples to unload further aid collected by the Soviet relief organizations.

Berlinguer invited the regional secretaries of the Party to form a welcoming committee to prepare for the arrival of the helicopters' crews. 'We shall do it in such a way that our visiting comrades will take back with them an unforgettable memory of the warm reception they received,' he proposed.

On returning to their respective towns in the south, the Communist leader repeated the happy news to their Party cadres. 'At last,' announced the secretary of the Salerno section, 'we won't have to go red in the face at the sight of all the American, English and French relief. So far the Soviet Union has appeared unresponsive to the catastrophe that has caused the death of thousands of our comrades and the loss of hundreds of thousands of workers' homes in southern Italy. We have seen too many priests in the ruins of our houses, and it is only right that a comforting gesture also comes from Moscow.'

The Communists of Mercato San Severino, a town on the outskirts of Avellino, decided that their section would assume the honorary name of the first Soviet pilot to transport Russian aid to that area.

A small local foundry, only slightly damaged by the tremors, was commissioned to make a bronze commemorative medal to present to the Soviet helicopters' crews.

The Italian Transport Minister, in the meantime, received an official communication from the Soviet Embassy giving the arrival time of the aid from the USSR. Transport by helicopter would begin on Saturday 13 December, soon after the arrival of the naval convoy in the Tyrrhenian Sea, and would continue throughout the following days until unloading was completed.

The official of the Ministry in charge of the supervision of the airlift quickly granted permission for the proposed flight of the Soviet helicopters in Italian skies.

Under normal circumstances the request presented by the Embassy of the USSR would have been looked upon with suspicion and probably rejected, but this time considerations of a humanitarian nature called for an exception. Undoubtedly the Communist Party would exploit the arrival of Soviet help in the devastated provinces for political ends. But the Italian Socialists had already launched a propaganda campaign for the help sent by the Bonn Social Democratic Chancellor Schmidt; the Christian Democrats had shown their jubilation at the arrival of American relief; the Liberals had applauded the reception of the caravans sent by the British Conservative Government, and so on. 'The politicians succeed in speculating on even the most terrible of disasters,' thought the civil servant, while approving the document headed 'Soviet Measures for the Earthquake Victims'.

However, in an excess of prudence, the Ministry official wanted to inform the Italian Military Counterespionage Service of the imminent arrival of the Soviet helicopters. The signal was received by a colonel who immediately consulted his superiors.

The officers were inclined to dismiss the idea that the helicopters' mission was one of espionage. 'Soviet satellites fly permanently over our heads and are able to photograph even the pants we wear under our trousers. Moreover, the Russian diplomats are not so stupid as to ask official permission for covert undertakings,' said one of them in a tone which would not allow for objection.

'But the helicopters could transport illegal weapons for the Red Brigades besides help for the earthquake victims,' the colonel surmised.

'Do you think that the administrators in the Kremlin would risk a scandal while their Italian comrades are publicizing Soviet aid for southern Italy?'

A general took a copy of a Communist newspaper from a drawer in his desk, on the front page of which a headline of six columns was dedicated to the 'Generous Initiative of the USSR for the Victims of the Earthquake'.

'At any rate,' added the general, 'in the interests of national security we had better keep an eye on them. We will ask the Soviet Embassy for a detailed list of all goods transported by the helicopters and then have the loads checked scrupulously on arrival at Salerno, Avellino and Potenza. The unloading at Naples will be checked by the harbour police.'

Capri

The portraits of Karl Liebknecht and Rosa Luxemburg, heroes of the Spartacus League, who were killed by the German police in 1919, decorated the walls of Frau Ursula Riesman's bedroom. She was born in Berlin in 1923 and became a KGB agent during the Second World War, when she was left the young widow of a wealthy Austrian architect. Frau Ursula established herself on Capri in 1952, opening a little boutique with the money she received from the sale of her husband's estate, and automatically became the 'Capri resident' of the Soviet espionage machine.

The importance of the service that she had rendered to the KGB since the Stalin era, under the command of Beria, can be deduced from the fact that Frau Ursula was secretly conferred with honorary Soviet citizenship.

To the occasional visitor she would show the portraits of Karl Liebknecht and 'Rote Rosa' (Rosa the Red) implying that they were her maternal aunt and uncle, of whose memory she was especially fond. Although an atheist, she celebrated every Christmas, placing a rose before the picture of her supposed aunt, whose birthday was remembered on 25 December.

As the Western centre of the jet set, Capri had assumed a particular importance for the KGB in the fifties. Strolling in the Piazzetta of an evening it was possible to meet industrialists, politicians, scientists, trade unionists and writers from all countries, and to eavesdrop on their conversations while sitting, elbow to elbow, at the little tables.

A more profitable occupation was found frequenting the villas of the international aristocrats on the Marina Piccola, where one ran across such people as von Bohlen und Halbach of the Krupp dynasty, Agnelli of Fiat, Aristotle Onassis and other private shipowners; ministers in office and former ministers; admirals and generals in service or retired.

When she transferred to Capri, Frau Ursula Riesman gained

entry into that exclusive and insular society, whose members only welcomed to their homes visitors of special value, encouraging their caprices and illicit love affairs, knowing how to make their days and nights enjoyable. At that time she was an attractive, glamorous woman in her thirties, available for other people's pleasure. For her best friends she would sacrifice the graces and the virtues of the charming models who regularly patronized her boutique. On more than one occasion the little villa on the Via Tuoro had welcomed lively groups who had disported themselves throughout the night under the severe gaze of 'Uncle' Karl and 'Aunt' Rosa. Many times these encounters enabled Frau Ursula to gain useful information which she regularly passed on to a courier who came from Rome.

When she recalled to mind those years of intense activity, Frau Ursula had the strange sensation of passing through a long portrait gallery, along which the faces of the world's famous looked down at her from the walls; faces she had known for only an instant or for many hours. Some of those faces had become very familar to her, while others had briefly crossed her path, quickly vanishing into nothing.

Through her boutique passed the wives of heads of state and of governments; princesses; actresses and opera singers whom the public had frenziedly acclaimed. She had shaken hands with Jacqueline Kennedy, with the princesses of Savoia and Hohenzollern, with Greta Garbo and Brigitte Bardot, with Maria Callas . . . until the time when the international clientele began to desert Capri for the Bahamas and the Far East. Other islands, less accessible to the tourist masses, had become the poles of attraction for the jet set, who did not like staying in one place too long.

Capri had not lost that natural fascination which once beckoned to her shores those cosmopolitans of refined tastes such as Axel Munthe, Baron Jacques d'Adelsward-Fersen, Freidrich Krupp, the Fords, the Vanderbilts, and the Agnellis, some of whom had built villas still admired today for the architecture that blends so perfectly with the surroundings. The institution of the 'package tour' brought a different type of person to the island, wealthy but not aristocratic, who according to the one-time regular visitors only served to pollute the air. This is why some of these regulars had transferred their attention to other places, seeking relaxation away from the gaze of the 'vulgar'.

The debasement of Caprian tourism had, as a direct consequence, diminished the amount of savoury information available for the Soviet secret service. The activities of Frau Ursula were therefore reduced, and Rome headquarters sent a courier only when absolutely necessary, on the receipt of her usual signal. During the golden season of the fifties and sixties, the courier arrived regularly every month to sift through the information she had gathered in her boutique, in the Piazzetta, in the salons and in the beds of Capri.

But the passing years had also affected the rapacious capacity of Ursula Riesman, who was gradually left out of the parties which would have been most profitable to her hidden talents. She was becoming someone who was still formally invited but was not necessarily welcomed, although clever makeup disguised in part the encroachment of time. She became, in short, a type of 'gatecrasher' tolerated by her hosts, who were very often of the younger generation.

Nearing sixty, Frau Ursula decided to give up the management of the boutique and to close herself away in the small villa on the Via Tuoro, making an appearance only on special occasions. Her part in the KGB became that of a 'sleeping agent', who would be recalled into service only if the necessity arose.

Withdrawing into a private life, Frau Ursula ventured out regularly on a Sunday morning when she went to the piazza where, from a terrace overlooking the Marina Grande, she could see the arrival of the motor launches and hydrofoils loaded with the tourists who came to pour money into the life-blood of Capri. As the noisy groups of new arrivals passed in front of her, she thought how radically life on Capri had changed since she had taken up residence on the island.

The solitary visitors of one time, eager to climb up to Monte Solaro or to Villa Jovis quietly to enjoy the twin pleasures of art and nature, were now replaced by breathless, noisy groups, untidily trailing after their guides like flocks of sheep. Within a few hours they would see Capri and Anacapri, leaping from one place to another like frantic grasshoppers; they would then stop to buy souvenirs at shops already selected by those same guides who had been enlisted by the traders with promises of generous commissions on the amount of business transacted.

Staying at home, Frau Ursula read the newspapers and kept herself up to date on the movements of the famous in order to know when they would be coming to Capri. Many celebrated residents of the fifties had gone for good – Countess Ciano, daughter of the Fascist dictator Benito Mussolini and widow of Count Galeazzo, who was executed in Verona for high treason by those same Fascists; Bob Hornstein, the generous American host who had arranged such fantastic parties in his splendid villa in Via Tragara, had returned to the United States; Gracie Fields, the English singer, owner of the luxurious bathing establishment 'La Canzone del Mare', was dead, and sadly missed by her friends and admirers.

Ursula's telephone rarely rang now. She had never had children; a nephew who lived in Wiesbaden and worked in a bank would one day inherit the few possessions she owned, including the little villa in Via Tuoro. Perhaps to ascertain that the time had not yet come to think of his legacy, he would ring her once or twice a year to enquire after her health.

It was with understandable surprise that Frau Riesman received, in the first week of December 1980, a visit from a Rome courier who identified himself with the words: 'I bring you the best wishes of your Cousin Mathilde from Dortmund.' The same words had been used in earlier years when she had been on active service. She had replied now, as before: 'Which Mathilde?' and the other had clarified: 'Mathilde Brückner, the daughter of Gustav.' After a brief exchange of courtesies the courier said: 'We have to use your house for a couple of weeks.' She replied: 'Will it be necessary for me to move out?' 'No. You can stay. The important thing is that you have two beds available. In a few days you will receive two visitors. We would like you to help them in every way and also to keep an eye on them.' Frau Ursula knew that it would be useless to ask further questions. The courier would most probably be ignorant of the answers and, anyway, he would not give her an explanation if he had been instructed to the contrary.

Rome

The Soviet battle cruiser *Kirov* is the largest warship, other than aircraft carriers, to be built by any country since the Second World War. Western estimates put her displacement weight at 32,000 tons. She is armed with the latest anti-ship and anti-aircraft missiles and provided with space satellite communi-cations systems and expensive electronic countermeasures to jam enemy radar.

When asked to suggest the most suitable vessel for the secret meeting between John Paul II and Brezhnev, the Soviet Defence Minister, Marshal Ustinov, chose the *Kirov* without hesitation.

'But we can't invite the Pope on to a battleship', objected several members of the Politburo. Ustinov patiently explained that the *Kirov* offered the best guarantee of protection for the two heads of state if they wished to converse in a relaxed atmosphere, with no risk to their personal safety.

The cruiser had already arrived in the Mediterranean, escorted by the aircraft carrier *Kiev*, by two nuclear submarines, and by other surface vessels disguised as merchant ships. Operation Pilgrim, planned by Yuri Andropov in all its particulars, anticipated a constant link between the *Kirov* and the radio station installed by Natasha, with the help of Sergei, in the Caprian villa of Frau Ursula.

During the stay of Brezhnev and his 'guest' on the ship, Natasha would maintain permanent contact from Capri with an officer of the *Kirov* expert in telecommunications, while Sergei would remain telephonically linked with the Soviet Embassy in Rome. At the same time an 'open line' via satellite between the Kremlin and the *Kirov* would permit the Soviet President to be informed of any event on the national or international scene.

The arrival of Brezhnev and the Pope on the cruiser would take place at two different times. After having reached the

71

Kiev by plane, the President of the USSR would transfer to the *Kirov* at a preselected moment and prepare to receive the head of the Catholic Church. John Paul II would arrive by helicopter soon after.

This plan had been prepared to the last detail, and Yuri Andropov, responsible for its supervision from Rome, could consider himself satisfied. The first report sent from Capri by Natasha and Sergei confirmed that the trial link-up with the *Kirov* had been carried out without difficulty and that the ship was ready for Operation Pilgrim. But 'Day X' could only be decided by Moscow when the Pope had shown himself to be agreeable to a secret encounter with Brezhnev.

For the first time in the history of international relations, a high-level discussion had been arranged with the maximum secrecy by one of the two participants without the knowledge of the other.

Andropov could not exclude the possibility of an unexpected counter-order annulling the plan, should the Pope reject the invitation or refuse to agree to the site of the meeting suggested by Moscow.

The responsibility of the chief of the KGB was limited to the executive stage of the project. Foreign Minister Gromyko had assumed the task of personally taking Brezhnev's invitation to the Pope, for the purpose of carrying out an intense effort of persuasion to induce him to accept.

But even Gromyko's mission was not free from obstacles. The Soviet Minister had to come incognito into the presence of the Pope to avoid arousing a clamour of international public opinion. In this connection Andropov proposed a move, on the result of which would depend the success of the operation.

Gromyko should arrive, preferably, at Castel Gandolfo by the same helicopter that would later take John Paul II to the *Kirov*. In this way the eventual acceptance of the invitation by the Pontiff would immediately be followed by the execution of the plan, before the Vatican counsellors could even attempt to impede the meeting with Brezhnev.

Theoretically, no one could prevent the Pope from

absenting himself for a few hours from the pontifical residence for the purpose of once again going to visit the disaster areas in the south. The helicopter which Gromyko would have at his disposal was able to reach the *Kirov* in about an hour – as the crow flies – a lot quicker than going from Rome to Salerno, Avellino or Potenza.

The Italian Minister of Transport had agreed that the Soviet helicopters would adopt the insignia of the International Red Cross during the transportation of relief for the earthquake victims. Therefore, no one would be surprised if, for some unexpected reason, the Pope was seen getting into such a helicopter.

The secret visit of the Soviet Foreign Minister required extreme caution in its organization, precisely because of the consequences that could arise from such a meeting.

Most important of all it had to be arranged in such a manner that the Pope would grant Gromyko an audience at Castel Gandolfo and not at the Vatican, in order to ensure secrecy.

During the summer season it is quite normal for the Pope to receive important visitors at his country residence, which is situated 30 kilometres south-east of Rome. The villa was built by Carlo Maderno on the instructions of Pope Urban VIII, who liked to be surrounded by artists and who wrote poetry in both Latin and Italian. Construction began in 1626 and the villa was later remodelled by Bernini. Since the Lateran Treaty of 1929, it has been considered by the Italian Government as an extraterritorial possession of the Holy See – as part of the Vatican City.

The last foreign statesman to be received by the Pope at Castel Gandolfo in the summer of 1980 was King Hussein of Jordan. This visit took place on 1 September and photographs of that meeting were printed in the newspapers of many countries. But Gromyko wanted to go to Castel Gandolfo in December – that is, in the middle of winter, which the Pontiff usually spent in the Apostolic Palace in Rome. The inexhaustible Andropov devised a strategy to secure even this objective.

Vatican City

The Secretary of State, Cardinal Agostino Casaroli, administered the foreign affairs of the Catholic Church from his austere office on the first loggia of the Apostolic Palace.

A diplomat by training, Casaroli began to emerge from the ranks of the Vatican State secretariat in 1961 when John XXIII sent him to Vienna to attend a convention on consular relations organized by the United Nations.

From that time he dedicated himself to the development of relations between the Holy See and the Communist governments of Eastern Europe. The problem was made particularly complex by the presence of some sixty million European Catholics subject to Marxist rule. Pope Paul VI continued to make use of the acumen and adaptability of Casaroli in dealing with Eastern statesmen, entrusting to him the delicate missions that have contributed to the improvement, within the limits possible, of the ministry of the so-called 'silent church'.

During his visits to Poland, Casaroli met the then Cardinal Wojtyla several times, and their friendship was strengthened during the last stage of the Second Vatican Council in the 1970s. To the experts in ecclesiastical affairs it was no surprise that Casaroli obtained the nomination of Secretary of State from John Paul II as soon as the position became vacant.

After succeeding the French Cardinal Villot, the first change Casaroli made was to transfer the office of the Secretary of State from the second to the first loggia, thus bringing it down by one floor. Spiteful tongues muttered that he had done this in order to make a quick departure – being nearer to St Peter's Square – when work became too burdensome.

After the reform of the Roman Curia in 1967, the Secretary of State became the chief coordinator for various departments of the Holy See. Acting as the Prefect of the Council for Public Affairs of the Church, the body responsible for the Vatican diplomatic service, Cardinal Casaroli controls the daily diplomatic activity carried out by the nuncios or apostolic delegates in more than a hundred countries, many non-Catholic and sometimes even non-Christian, such as Yugoslavia and various countries of the Middle East where the Vatican is officially represented.

A permanent observer of the Holy See sits on the General Assembly of the United Nations, and obviously the Secretary of State has to follow the vicissitudes of the Catholics even in those countries that do not recognize the Vatican and oppose its action on an international level.

These many duties cover Casaroli's desk with a mountain of files to read or letters to sign, while in the anteroom visiting clergy and civil diplomats of all nationalities arrive continuously.

On the morning of Tuesday 9 December 1980, the Cardinal Secretary of State received an unusual telephone call. The chargé d'affaires of the Soviet Embassy in Prague, Wladimir Mironov, was passing through Rome and wished to see him personally to give him a little gift.

Casaroli had met the slender Mironov many years before in Budapest, when the Catholic Church was involved in the difficult negotiations to allow the departure of Cardinal Mindszenty from Hungary. Highly thought of by the hierachy of the Kremlin, Mironov was – according to Khrushchev's amusing definition – 'a diplomat who would pass unseen even if he walked with two bells hanging around his neck'.

'I will see you with pleasure if you are not afraid to cross the bronze doors of the Vatican. How long are you staying in Rome?' asked Casaroli while glancing through his full diary.

'I must leave tomorrow night at the latest. But what I have for you is perishable.'

'If that is so, then come at once. I will try and fit you in between two other engagements.'

A few moments before midday, Mironov was introduced into Casaroli's office and greeted him warmly – like a long-lost friend.

75

The Russian took from his leather briefcase a jar of caviar and placed it on the table, saying: 'This is the little gift; however, the perishable one is something else.' The Cardinal accepted the caviar with a smile while trying to understand Mironov's meaning. 'May I offer you something to drink?' he asked.

'I am here on a special mission,' said Mironov, ignoring the offer, 'and I hope that you will cooperate with me.'

'What does it concern?' the Cardinal enquired.

'An airlift of the brotherhood will be set up next Sunday between the Soviet merchant fleet and the Italian regions damaged in the earthquake. Several Soviet helicopters will fly to and fro between our vessels and the most stricken towns, transporting all kinds of relief.'

'A worthy gesture,' interrupted Casaroli. 'The newspapers have written about it and the Holy Father will express, in a future homily, his appreciation to the Government in Moscow for this humanitarian act.'

'I have come to confide in you that the Minister of Foreign Affairs, Gromyko, wants to take advantage of these circumstances to deliver personally, and in absolute secrecy, a message from President Brezhnev to the Holy Father.'

'Do you mean that Gromyko proposes to come to Rome?'

'He will, if the Pope is disposed to grant him a private audience, devoid of all forms of publicity. To this end, the Government of the USSR would like to suggest that the visit takes place at Castel Gandolfo, where one of the helicopters flying towards the south could easily be diverted without attracting too much attention.'

Casaroli managed with difficulty to contain his surprise.

'But is it really necessary that the Minister sees the Pontiff and that the meeting is arranged in such a hurry?'

'More than necessary – it is of the utmost importance,' said Mironov, with studied slowness.

'You understand that I am not able to give any assurance of an audience taking place, but I will deliver the request of your Government to the Holy Father immediately. Can you at least advise me of the reason for this proposed visit?'

76

'I would already have done so if I knew. I am only aware that Brezhnev intends to consult the Pope before announcing an imminent initiative which could have immediate and important repercussions on peaceful coexistence between the people!'

'You have still not said if you will have something to drink,' observed Casaroli, perplexed.

'Do not worry, thank you. We will drink a toast on some other occasion. Tell me rather, when can I have an answer?'

'From your impatience I deduce that Moscow is extremely anxious to arrange this meeting. Let me look at His Holiness's diary of official duties. Sunday 14 December – there is a pontifical visit in the afternoon to the Roman parish of the Nativity in the Appio Latino district, but no official engagements are foreseen for the evening.'

'The instructions I have received indicate that Minister Gromyko can come to the Pope at any hour providing that visibility is suitable for the helicopter's landing.'

'I understand. I will confer with His Holiness and let you know the answer as soon as possible. How can I contact you?'

If you don't mind, I will ring you from a public telephone to ask when delivery of the perishable gift can be arranged. You will only have to mention the time.'

'I hope to have the answer in a couple of hours.'

Mironov took his leave with the same effusion he had shown on arrival.

Capri

Sergei and Natasha intended that their Capri mission should also be their honeymoon. They knew they would remain on the island for only a few days, as Operation Pilgrim had to be put into action as quickly as possible to have any chance of success. Within the turn of a week at the maximum, they would receive orders to dismantle the radio station and return to Rome. The directive issued by Yuri Andropov in fact anticipated that the operation would succeed or fail within the first half of December.

Each morning the couple contacted headquarters for instructions. Sergei and Natasha took it in turns to use the public coin box in the Via Tragara, dialling the prefix 06 for Rome followed by six digits. The conversation lasted less than the telephone unit of three minutes.

'Has the cheque arrived?'

'Not yet. We hope to receive it today.'

This exchange of words was followed by casual remarks of a meteorological and social nature concerning the tranquil Capri winter.

The voice coming from Rome invariably asked after the health of the two and hoped they would have a happy holiday. Radio contact was made each day between Capri and the cruiser *Kirov*, transmitting news that, to a foreign ear, would be considered idle and without interest.

Work occupied only a fraction of their time, as frequently happens when a secret agent is forced to await instructions in a place cut off from the events for which he was mobilized.

Sergei and Natasha were temporarily filed away in an 'empty letter-box', according to KGB jargon; they tried to take advantage of this situation in the best possible way – on a personal basis – until the arrival of the message that would bring them into total activity.

With the senses she was given, Frau Ursula was not slow to

realize that the bond between the couple was not limited to the service of the KGB, although Sergei and Natasha did everything possible to hide their liaison. Frau Ursula had prepared two separate rooms on the first floor of the villa, but certain sounds and movements during the night convinced her that perhaps a double room would have been more convenient. Frau Ursula was also aware of the strict regulations that forbade two agents embarking on an affair during the performance of their duty, and she asked herself why her guests should be so foolhardy as to risk being denounced to their superiors. Probably they loved each other, but experience had taught her that it was precisely in these passionate affairs that a good agent must exercise the utmost self-control, putting aside every temptation. The golden rule of Frau Ursula had always been: 'Love for reasons of duty at any time of the day or night; love against the interests of duty – never!'

So as not to be considered an unwanted third party, Frau Ursula declined their invitation to accompany them on their walks, but she suggested some delightful and charming excursions they should take the better to appreciate the beauties of the island.

Visitors to Capri should not miss admiring those obligatory sights such as the Blue Grotto, the natural arch, or Monte Solaro. On the advice of Frau Ursula the two KGB agents went to see all these places, as well as visiting the Certosa monastery and climbing down along the rocky ridge that projects steeply from Tragara Point to the Faraglioni. As well as the Blue Grotto they saw the Green Grotto and the Monk's Grotto – so called because the formation of a limestone outgrowth resembles a monk in prayer. On leaving, the boatman who had taken them to the Blue Grotto wished them good health and sons, according to the custom of the old Capri generation who considered that only sons were able to attain riches, adventuring out onto the sea as fishermen or as sailors on merchant ships.

To reach the top of Monte Solaro they had first to leave

Capri for Anacapri by one of the small buses that the Comune ran on the island's slope – open to a limited amount of motor traffic. Sergei was impressed at the ability of the Caprian drivers to speed along winding, narrow roads with only a millimetre of space between their vehicles and the oncoming traffic, without ever causing an accident. He asked himself how it was that the Soviet Union, which produces some of the finest athletes in the world, has never excelled in motor racing, but he could find no logical explanation apart from the fact that the biggest motor industries are located in the West.

From Anacapri they took the chairlift up to Monte Solaro, and from professional scruples also took the precaution of going separately. 'If the cable breaks, it would be better if only one of us finishes up in hospital with a broken leg. The boss would never forgive a mistake like that,' Sergei had thought.

The view from Monte Solaro extends far out across the sea to the plains of the Sorrentine peninsula. Natasha abandoned herself to a rapture which made her feel even closer to Sergei, and she tried to convey her devotion to him.

One afternoon they were caught in a storm while visiting Villa Jovis and took shelter among the ruins under an ancient arch, waiting for the rain to stop. Natasha pressed herself against Sergei, her arms holding him close. 'Oh, I wish this storm would never end!' she cried.

'You like this lousy weather?' he asked in surprise.

'It's the first time we can be really close together during the day.'

Sergei quickly veered the conversation away from the sentimental. 'Did you know that the Emperor Tiberius used to spend his summers here during the last ten years of his life? He built no fewer than twelve villas on Capri and named all of them after deities. This is the most beautiful – that is why it is named after the chief Roman god. I read all that in a guidebook.'

'Could I ask Jove to protect my love for you?'

'A pagan god would never accept the prayers of a Soviet girl,' he laughed.

80

The rain continued to fall and flashes of lightning cut across the leaden sky. They stood silently watching the elements, their arms around each other.

The idyllic atmosphere was only broken when Sergei, turning her face towards him, suddenly asked: 'Was there anything between you and Andropov?'

Natasha looked at him a long while before replying with another question: 'And if there was?'

He shrugged. 'Just curious. You are perfectly free to do what you want.'

'If you are referring to his wish to see Rome by night, we walked around Trastevere for hours. He wanted to meet the common people of the city: he stopped at each street stall; I had to ask them about their earnings and their family life. Then we went to eat in a typical Roman restaurant.'

'Interesting. And then . . .?'

'Then . . . nothing. I took him to sample the hot roasts on the Piazza Navona and then accompanied him to the Ambassasdor's residence.'

'Did he ask you to stay with him?'

'Don't be indiscreet. I stayed only for a drink. Is the interrogation over?'

'Sure – if you like; in any case I won't check up on you.'

'Let's go down,' she said, a chill in her voice. 'I'm cold now.' A shaft of sunlight broke through the black clouds and the rain ceased.

During their stay they ate at either Gemma's or the Gatto Bianco, where the old guitarist, Scarola, sang classic Neapolitan songs, and as these were repeated many times Sergei and Natasha soon began to learn and understand the words in dialect. The song she preferred, perhaps because it best described her state of mind, was 'Luna Caprese'. Sergei liked the livelier tunes, such as 'Funiculi, funicula'. The closeness that Natasha felt for him was assuming proportions that neither desired; she began to dread the moment when they would again have to part – perhaps for ever. Sergei was frequently distant and almost unapproachable, though at the same time letting her see that he was fond of her. On the completion of the mission he would return to his wife and quickly forget her.

The bathing establishments on the Marina Piccola were closed during the winter, and they were therefore able to go beyond the deserted cabins to the rocks. On sunny days they felt the urge to dive into the sea, but the call of duty advised them to avoid the risk of catching cold.

The momentary relaxation of the spirit and senses to which they had abandoned themselves was suddenly brought to an end on the morning of Thursday 11 December during the daily telephone conversation with Rome. The cheque had finally arrived, and uncle was going to deposit it in the bank the following day. This message meant that Operation Pilgrim was about to begin.

Castel Gandolfo

Late in the afternoon of 14 December 1980, Karol Wojtyla 'the son of the Polish people called to guide the Universal Church' (a description he has publicly given himself) awaited the visit of Andrei Gromyko at Castel Gandolfo. The whole morning had been spent in carrying out the exhausting duties that occur daily in the life of a Pope who, because of the nature of his ministry, is – according to the words of Paul VI – destined to rest only after death.

As the 264th successor to Peter, the first non-Italian Pope for 455 years, and the first Polish Pope in the history of the Catholic Church, John Paul II also became, with his election on 16 October 1978, the Bishop of Rome, Patriarch of the West, Primate of Italy, Archbishop and Metropolitan of the Province of Rome, and Sovereign of the Vatican State.

These duties were handed down from one Vicar of Christ to the next, but the pontifical style changed according to the person invested. The Church has had austere popes and merry popes, introvert and extrovert popes, learned popes and popes fired by the simple wisdom of their country parishes. In past centuries there were also sinner popes, who were besmirched with every type of crime, when the temporal power of the Church manifested itself in territorial acquisitions, intrigues and wars.

On the day of his inauguration the Pope followed the innovation of his predecessor and refused to wear the Tiara – that ancient symbol of temporal power. Speaking to the heads of state, to the representatives of governments, to the cardinals and to the crowds gathered around him, he presented himself as 'the servant of the unique, sweet power of Christ'. And calling upon Christ, added: 'Make me a servant. Indeed, the servant of your servants.'

The talks that followed and the visits the Pontiff made

around the world showed that he dedicated a major part of his energies to the great cause of ecumenism and universal peace, which could only come about through better understanding between the peoples.

As written in the Book of Genesis, the Supreme Shepherd, 'ready to lay down His life for His sheep', would not hesitate for an instant to go out in the cold to search for a lost sheep. And having found the sheep 'would lay it across his shoulders rejoicing' and return it to the flock – according to St Luke the Evangelist.

Immediately after his inauguration, the Pope spoke to journalists gathered in the hall of the Consistory. One of them asked: 'Holy Father, would you like to visit Russia?' and he replied: 'When they will let me.'

Remembering these words, the Cardinal Secretary of State, Agostino Casaroli, was not at all surprised when John Paul II declared that he was not only disposed but also happy to receive Gromyko in a private audience at Castel Gandolfo. The reason for the visit was not known to Casaroli, but the Head of the Catholic Church was not afraid of the unknown: 'Do not be afraid of toil: be afraid only of thoughtlessness and pusillanimity.'

To compliment his guest, the Pope ordered that the traditional tokens of Polish hospitality – bread and salt – be prepared.

While awaiting the visit he meditated and prayed for a long time, entrusting to Christ, and to the Holy Mother of Czestochowa – whom he had venerated since infancy – the future of the Church and the world. In his mind he repeated the words of the Polish hymn which says 'Tomorrow depends on You'.

To be near him in this situation Casaroli had also gone to Castel Gandolfo.

The sparkling winter's day had been warmed by a brilliant sun, now sinking towards dusk. Walking in the gardens of the pontifical country residence, close to the heliport, the Pope repeated the Psalm of David:

I will love thee, O Lord, my strength.
The Lord is my rock, and my fortress, and
my deliverer; my God, my strength, in whom
I will trust; my buckler, and the horn of
my salvation, and my high tower . . .

To protect himself from the cold, John Paul II had put on a lambswool cardigan over his cassock; he had done so mainly to satisfy the Polish 'sister servants of the Sacred Heart' who ran his household and were permanently concerned for his health.

Born in Wadowice on 18 May 1920, the Pope enjoyed robust health which would have enabled him still to ski in the Tatra Mountains or to take a canoe out on the beautiful lakes of his country, if the inscrutable designs of Providence had not called him to the Holy See.

To keep physically fit he had an indoor swimming pool installed at Castel Gandolfo, where he swam when cirumstances permitted. On this December day he had had to forego his swim as his Soviet guest could arrive at any time, so he was confined to walking along the avenues in the garden, accompanied by his Secretary of State. Several times they strolled the short distance separating the Observatory from the Theatre of Domitian, whose semicircular steps were crumbling away and in need of patient restoration.

In deep conversation on the Church's international affairs, they came to that part of the garden which is divided into flowery terraces, falling away towards a rustic area where there is a small farm. Although he was deeply involved in his discussion the Pope did not fail to admire the work of the gardeners, who kept constant order among the flowers, the cypresses, the tall trees and the sculptured boxwood hedges. The calm was suddenly broken by the noisy arrival of two helicopters, which circled over the residence for a few moments before starting the descent on the heliport. Followed by Casaroli, the Pope strode rapidly towards the landing place.

Both the helicopters bore the insignia of the International Red Cross. The first to touch down was that of the escort. The two men climbed out hurriedly and placed themselves in a position to supervise the landing of the other machine. From the second helicopter a figure emerged – unmistakably that of Gromyko – in a dark coat and with his head uncovered. He descended with the help of his aides as the Pope came to meet him, both hands outstretched in greeting.

'I am happy to see you again,' he said, speaking in Russian, 'and I hope that you have had a good journey.' They had met in Poland five years before, during the celebrations of the thirtieth anniversary of the end of the Second World War. At that time Karol Wojtyla was Cardinal of Cracow, and Gromyko had already broken a world record by holding the post of Minister of Foreign Affairs for the longest uninterrupted time; by 1980 he had been in office for twenty-three years.

Gromyko exchanged the Pope's greeting with deferential effusion, and then warmly shook Casaroli's hand. 'The journey was very good though a little tiring. As you know, I accompanied President Brezhnev on the official visit to India, which only ended two days ago – I stopped in Moscow long enough to repack my case.'

The Pope led his guest to the rear entrance of the villa that opened out onto the gardens. 'Tell me about your President. There has been some worrying news about his health in the past few months.'

'He has fully resumed his duties, though he must look after his health with greater care. I have been sent here by him, and am to say, Holiness, that he anxiously awaits the outcome of my mission.' Spoken by Gromyko, the title of 'Holiness' seemed a blasphemy as it implied, no doubt involuntarily, a sarcasm.

Turning to Casaroli, Gromyko added: 'I must thank your Eminence for your kind mediation.'

They entered a small reception room where a fire burned. Gromyko, smiling, held his hands out to the blaze in order to warm them. From the walnut table in the centre of the room the Pope took a small silver dish containing the two symbols of bread and salt, and offered it to his guest, saying: 'Welcome to this house of the Lord.'

They sat on either side of the fireplace in two green brocade armchairs while Casaroli sat on a sofa of the same colour placed against one of the walls, on which hung a bronze crucifix; on the wall opposite were two sixteenth-century paintings representing the patron saints of Italy – St Francis of Assisi and St Catherine of Siena.

'You will not refuse a cup of tea, blended by our Polish sisters and prepared in a Russian samovar?' offered the Pope.

'With pleasure,' replied Gromyko. 'Mrs Gandhi offered us Indian tea and I must confess that it was not to my taste.'

'Your long experience as Foreign Minister will have made you a connoisseur of the food and drink of all countries,' observed Casaroli. The Cardinal spoke in French, for although he understood Russian he had not mastered that language.

'Before the beginning of your pontificate I counted myself as being the most active traveller in the world, but you, Holiness, have put me in the shade with your incessant comings and goings.'

The Secretary of State withdrew discreetly from the room as the Pope carefully brought the conversation towards the reason for this visit. 'I am told that you have come to Italy to supervise the transport of Soviet aid to the areas hit by the earthquake. I visited these areas a few days ago and I can tell you that the sight is heartbreaking. Every gesture of help merits applause.'

'Holy Father, I do not intend going to southern Italy. I have come to Castel Gandolfo to tell you that President Brezhnev wishes to speak to you personally and with extreme urgency.'

'I am sorry that you have been troubled for this. I welcome any invitation that would improve relationships and communication between all people and all political institutions. Tell me where I can reach the President by telephone and I will call him immediately.'

'If you will permit me, Holiness,' interrupted Gromyko, holding up his hand, 'the situation is slightly different from

87

what you imagine. President Brezhnev has arrived incognito in the Mediterranean and asks that you join him, without delay, to discuss urgent problems upon which depends the peace of the world.'

'Are you referring to the problems of my country?'

'Yes, and to many international questions which are closely connected. I beg you, Holy Father, to accept this invitation – in the interests of Poland and the world.'

'I have already proclaimed that a Polish Pope has the sacrosanct right to share in the joys, the worries, the pain and the sorrows of his own nation. If a meeting with President Brezhnev can contribute towards alleviating this adversity I am ready to cooperate. But where? Do not forget that even the Pope has a strict schedule to follow.'

'We knew you would accept. If you will allow yourself to be guided by me we can be on the ship where the President awaits you in less than an hour.'

'The successor of Peter is able to feel at home in any part of the globe – wherever his ministry calls him. But are you asking me to go secretly?'

'There is no other way to arrive at this meeting, Holiness. After having spent four days in India, President Brezhnev has left the Soviet Union in secret to meet you. The people of the Soviet Union are convinced that he is spending a little time resting at his dacha to recover from the strain of his journey to New Delhi.'

'We are unworthy servants in the hands of God. Allow me to pray for a short while.'

The Pope retired to his private chapel, leaving Gromyko to ponder the uncertainty. In the meantime tea was brought in and served; Gromyko took the cup handed to him and emptied it with enjoyment.

Twenty minutes later the Pope returned, leading Casaroli by the hand. The Cardinal's face was ashen, betraying his fears. John Paul II had put on a white cloak and was carrying a small travelling case. 'Don't be afraid,' he said to his Secretary of State. 'It is necessary to have the courage to walk in a direction where no one has gone before, just as once Simon needed the courage to journey from the lake of Gennesaret in Galilee to Rome – a place unknown to him.'

'But what about your personal safety?' asked Casaroli.

'Do not worry. Our guest has assured me that I will be back soon. And nothing would be better for a Pope than to die in the fulfilment of his ministry, in the service of humanity. Our times need an act of witness openly expressing the desire to bring nations and regimes closer together, as an indispensable condition for peace in this world.'

Together they went to the heliport, where the two helicopters were ready and waiting to take off. The Pope embraced Casaroli warmly before climbing into the helicopter, and added: 'If anyone asks about my absence, say that the Pope is carrying out his duty elsewhere, faithful to the motto, *Totus tuus.*'

Gromyko shook Casaroli by the hand and followed the Pope on board. 'Believe me, there is nothing to worry about. The Pontiff will be our guest for a few hours and we will take very good care of him.'

As the helicopter lifted into the air the Cardinal fell to his knees, his hands clasped, fervently murmuring: '*Fiat voluntas tua.*'

The Pope, meanwhile, had taken a Bible from his case which he opened at the Book of Genesis, where is written: 'We shall go towards the future!'

Capri

Radio communication between the villa in Via Tuoro and the cruiser *Kirov* intensified with the onset of Operation Pilgrim. If any message had been intercepted by a foreign power it would not, even if decoded, have revealed its true significance. The smokescreen created by the distribution of Soviet aid to the earthquake zones of southern Italy was used to advantage by the KGB to cover the presence of President Brezhnev and Foreign Minister Gromyko in the Mediterranean.

The radio bridge linking Capri with the *Kirov* was apparently necessary for the transport of relief coming from the USSR, its consignment to the selected towns and its distribution to the homeless victims. The decoding key was shown only to half a dozen people, including the head of the KGB, Yuri Andropov, who was personally supervising the development of the operation.

On Saturday 13 December the *Kirov* transmitted to Capri a long list of goods, medicines, equipment and other urgent supplies that were being carried by Soviet vessels in the Mediterranean. Natasha and Sergei were delighted to know that Avellino would be receiving 201 pairs of men's shoes and 148 pairs of women's shoes – this meant that the two Soviet leaders had arrived safely from Moscow and were already on board the *Kirov*.

The mission of Gromyko to Castel Gandolfo was fraught with great uncertainty. No one knew whether the Minister would return to the *Kirov* alone or 'accompanied'. In the afternoon Natasha received a communication that a Soviet helicopter was going to land in Salerno with a consignment that included eighty-four tents equipped with the accessories needed to tether them to rocky, snow-covered terrain. This meant that Gromyko was nearing the Pontifical residence. His arrival at Castel Gandolfo was announced in a message received about an hour later; from then on suspense increased progressively until late into the night.

The tension shown by Natasha and Sergei when Operation Pilgrim was imminent was not lost on Frau Ursula, who, although she did not know what was happening, was aware that something was in the air. Trained by the KGB, she knew better than to ask questions about the radio messages received by the couple staying in her house. For reasons of security she confided herself to asking whether the radio communications had a 'clean cover', should any of the Italian security services become curious.

Natasha explained that everything was in order and functioning in such a manner as to dispel any suspicions that might be aroused. The Soviet Embassy was controlling the movements of the relief-bringing convoy from Capri, the Ministry of Transport in Rome had given temporary authorization for the helicopters of the Soviet navy to unload earthquake relief in three devastated areas – Salerno, Avellino and Potenza.

Outwardly everything was satisfactory, but Frau Ursula tried to imagine the background to Operation Pilgrim that was hidden from her. In almost thirty years of living on the island she had never been called upon to set up a radio station linked with the Soviet navy. Such an unusual event was surely due to some exceptional circumstance: but what? Maybe, under cover of earthquake relief, a Soviet naval expedition was rehearsing a landing in southern Italy. Having unbridled her imagination in that direction, Frau Ursula recalled how the landing of Allied troops on the beaches of Anzio opened up the heart of the Italian peninsula during the Second World War. In the event of a third world war, the Soviet fleet would be likely to launch an attack against the Tyrrhenian coast. The islands in the Gulf of Naples would become the buoys of the Red Army . . . She dreamed of one day seeing the red flags of the USSR flying on the summit of Monte Solaro and on the battlements of the old castle of Castiglione. Perhaps she would even attain the supreme joy of seeing a Europe completely taken over by Communism . . .

91

Huddled in an armchair in her sitting room, the 'Capri resident' of the KGB abandoned herself to these fantasies with a bottle of the local wine. She thought it would be hospitable to offer Natasha and Sergei some refreshment – for several hours they had been busily deciphering messages coming in from somewhere out at sea and transmitting them to headquarters in Rome. Frau Ursula uncorked a second bottle, which she placed on a tray together with two glasses. She lifted the tray and carefully carried it up the stairs to the communications room. She paused a moment at the top of the flight, from where she could hear the murmur of voices coming through the door at the end of the corridor; the words were indistinct but as she drew nearer Natasha's voice rang out excitedly: 'The Pilgrim helicopter is on its way!'

Tapping at the door, she entered as Sergei was hurriedly passing this information on to Rome, assuring the recipient at the other end of further news.

Depositing the tray, Frau Ursula asked if all was going according to plan. 'Perfectly,' said Natasha, while Sergei made a sign of victory with his two fingers.

The excitement displayed by the couple seemed excessive for a normal transfer of goods from sea to land. Frau Ursula, urged by curiosity, quietly entered an adjoining room and placed her ear against the wall. For the first time in her career she spied on her KGB colleagues, moved only by the simple desire to know what was going on. She picked up hushed words, whispered by Natasha and Sergei and then passed on by him to headquarters. Suddenly and clearly Natasha cried out: 'Docking executed!'

Frau Ursula tried to understand this exclamation. She thought it could mean that Russian astronauts had completed a manoeuvre in space over the Mediterranean, the reference to 'docking' that two spaceships had linked up, and the fleet was communicating the success of the operation. Such success for the USSR, assuming this was the reason, must be celebrated by an extra toast. She went down to the wine cellar and chose a third bottle, which she took back to her room; she poured the

92

wine and soon paid no further attention to the voices of Sergei and Natasha, which grew fainter and indistinct.

While she drank alone, buried in the depths of the armchair, she began to chafe with anger and envy at being held in ignorance of some new triumph for the fatherland of socialism, which was probably taking place at that very moment. In order not to break one of the iron rules of the service – the trust of discretion every KGB agent has to be aware of and to possess – she had not dared to ask Natasha and Sergei for an explanation. Pouring more wine, she meditated upon the sharp contrast in behaviour between herself – who scrupulously carried out Moscow's directives, being an honorary citizen of the USSR – and her two guests, both Russian born, who brazenly infringed regulations by their sexual relationship.

She considered that in hiding from her the true significance of Operation Pilgrim, Natasha and Sergei were at fault while appearing to obey regulations. Evidently they considered her to be untrustworthy, and for that she would repay them as they deserved.

As the contents of the bottle diminished, so Frau Ursula became more and more resentful. She would teach them a lesson, that pair who did not trust her, but her schemes became confused by a progressive dulling of the senses as one glass followed another; she leaned her head against the back of the armchair, her eyelids drooped, and she dozed. As she slept, Operation Pilgrim entered its critical phase.

On Board the Kirov (1)

'Welcome to Soviet territory, Pope Jan Pawel.' With these words Leonid Ilyich Brezhnev greeted the arrival of John Paul II on board the cruiser *Kirov*. He addressed his visitor pronouncing his pontifical name in the Polish tongue.

'I would have preferred meeting you elsewhere and in better circumstances,' the Pope replied in Russian.

'I am sorry to have been forced to ask for this meeting with such urgency and secrecy.'

'I do not doubt that the President of the USSR has his own good reasons for taking such an initiative, and that is why I have accepted the invitation. I have already proclaimed my wish to be the servant of humanity, or, better, the servant of servants.'

During this exchange, Brezhnev had led the Pontiff towards the cabin in which the talk would take place. The Pope glanced around him with interest. The helicopter had been lowered into the bowels of the ship on an elevator and as soon as the Pope and Gromyko had alighted, it was raised again on its platform to the upper deck. An officer of the Soviet marines, his uniform covered in medals, awaited them on the threshold of the cabin; he brought himself rigidly to attention on seeing them coming along the gangway. Instinctively, the Pontiff raised his arm in a blessing, but stopped in time and instead gave a slight wave of the hand in greeting.

The white-walled cabin was comfortably but simply furnished. A dark leather couch and three easy chairs stood around a circular table on which was a telephone, writing paper and pens. A small drinks bar beside the table held bottles and glasses.

'Vodka and water,' Brezhnev indicated, 'all that is required to enable one to talk freely. The vodka comes from Moscow but the mineral water is Polish.'

94

'I know the spring it was drawn from,' said the Pope, reading the label.

Gromyko had respectfully remained in the background, following a step behind, as they walked along the gangway. When they reached the cabin he said: 'Your Holiness, please excuse me if I now leave. My job was to escort you to your destination and I hope I have done so in the best possible way.'

'In a very persuasive way,' was the reply.

'I will, of course, be ready to accompany you on your return to Castel Gandolfo. I shall advise Secretary of State Casaroli – through our Embassy in Rome – of your safe arrival.'

'We will formally assure him that the USSR has no intention of kidnapping the Supreme Pontiff,' added Brezhnev, jokingly.

The Pope forced a slight smile: 'Every pontificate has its chains.'

Gromyko withdrew, leaving the two leaders, for the first time, alone – face to face. The Dove was now in the Bear's den and studied him closely, gauging his intentions and testing his animal strength.

Under the bushy eyebrows the face of the Soviet President was strained and tense.

'I thank you for sharing the risk I am running by being here in the Mediterranean as a clandestine tourist. This sea is treacherous for the Soviet navy.'

'There is no fear for one who places himself in the hands of Christ,' replied the Pontiff.

'Those are the same words you spoke during your inaugural ceremony in St Peter's Square.'

'It is true. That day I exhorted my faithful brothers not to be afraid and to open their hearts to Jesus Christ. With the same conviction I desire that the heads of state would open their frontiers to Christ so that He may speak freely to all people. Only Christ can speak of life and hope.'

'Pope Jan Pawel, I have not asked you here to give me a sermon. I want to talk to you about the Polish question, which threatens the destiny of the entire human race.'

'Your words, Mr President, betray great worries. Permit me to say to you also: Do not be afraid.' Assisted by Brezhnev, the Pontiff removed his cloak and placed it on the couch before seating himself at the table.

'For our convenience, I propose that an interpreter is present,' said the Soviet President. 'Any misunderstandings between us could have incalculable consequences.'

'The Pope is not afraid as he has nothing to hide. However, I would prefer an informal conversation which would allow us to open our hearts to each other. If my knowledge of the Russian language does not appear to be adequate, I will attempt to speak in Ukranian – your mother tongue.'

'I know that we were born close to each other,' observed Brezhnev. 'Your Wadowice is only a few hundred kilometres from my Komenskoje. At least geographically we were made to understand each other. But I would not want to repeat anything to the Politburo that was not absolutely correct. If you agree I will make a few notes during our discussion: it was really for this purpose that I thought an interpreter would be useful, but I will do it myself. I don't want to get up to the tricks of President Nixon, who treacherously taped his visitors' words. With regard to your knowledge of the Russian language, I must compliment you. For the first time we have a polyglot Pope who can make himself understood both in the East and in the West. Unfortunately, the Polish I learned with the liberating Red Army in 1945 has grown rusty over the years. There were no problems between Poland and Russia in those days – when we were fighting side by side against Nazism.'

'The history of my country is rich with oppressors disguised as liberators who, at times and in good faith, believed themselves to be deliverers,' objected the Pontiff.

'I remember the jubilation of the people who gathered to welcome the advancing 19th Army at Pronin, at Nowy Targ, at Gorny Duraiec. No Soviet citizen is unaware that Lenin also lived on Polish territory. It was he who, in 1913, presided over the Bolshevik conference at Poronin.'

'In 1913 I had not yet come into the world,' mused the Pope. *'Tempus fugit.'*

'I am older than you by fourteen years,' stated Brezhnev. 'While you were studying Latin in the Theological Seminary at Cracow, I was already fighting against the Third Reich.'

'Each one of us fights his battles according to God's will. Under the Nazi regime I worked in a quarry.'

Brezhnev began to recite:

'It is he who carries the power in his hands,
The Worker,
Hands are the landscape of the heart
Man opens his fingers when he has toiled enough.'

The Pope took it up.

'All roads lead straight to my heart.
Silence is again in the heart,
In the stone, in the tree . . .'

He passed a hand over his eyes as though to cancel out some memory, and added: 'I am happy, Mr President, that you have found time to read my verses.'

'The biographies of popes are my favourite reading,' responded Brezhnev, 'but I am convinced that Jan Pawel II is not aware of the vicissitudes of the builders of Communism.'

'I can prove that you are mistaken,' contradicted the Pope. 'As you have recalled, we spent our youth relatively close to each other. While you were receiving your diploma in engineering in the present-day town of Dneprodzerzhinsk, I was going to the gymnasium at Wadowice.'

'I know that you were considered a model student. You would certainly have been taught that the first foreign investors in the steel industry of Kamenskoja and the nearby centres on the right bank of the Dnepr were Poles, French and Belgians. But they invested only to enrich themselves – with

97

the indulgence of the tsarist family. My progenitors cried: "Who can get fat on a wage of thirteen roubles?"'

'You became a Communist so that your compatriots could satisfy the hunger of their bodies. I became a priest, above all, to satisfy the hunger of the spirit.'

'My real school was the Komsomol – the Soviet Youth Organization. I was sixteen when I joined in 1923. To be admitted to the ranks of the Communist Party I had to wait until 1931, although my application was entered in 1929. I think it is easier for a Polish citizen to become a priest than for a Soviet citizen to join the Communist Party.'

'Real religious faith does not recognize obstacles,' commented the Pope.

'Now I understand how, at the age of thirty-eight, you became the youngest bishop in Poland. Though do not forget that it would only have taken a State veto to negate the episcopal nomination. And if Karol Wojtyla had not become bishop, the Kremlin would not have found it necessary to consult a Polish Pope today.'

We might have had a Hungarian, or one from the Far East, or – why not – a Ukrainian? The roads where Providence leads are many. But you did not invite me here to discuss the outcome of the last Conclave.'

'The Communist Party of the Soviet Union does not object to the election of a Slav Pope. We may ask ourselves, should we prefer a Slav or a Chinese Pope? What hurts many Russians is that Jan Pawel is acting like an American Pope! I read with surprise the speech in which you stated that Poland is the east of the West not the west of the East. It is a statement that I, trained in the politics of concrete ideas, interpreted as a repudiation of your origin.'

'It is not the first time that the Pope's words have been misinterpreted. I have also been described as the Pope who came in from the cold. The successor of Peter cannot be identified with a particular place or with a particular season, much less with a political creed. He is the Shepherd of all peoples. The renunciation of the Tiara, introduced by my predecessor and perpetuated by me, symbolizes a separation from all forms of temporal power. Stalin jokingly asked how many divisions the Pope had available. The question was rhetorical and the answer has never changed: the Pope does not have and does not need any divisions in his service.'

'The Vatican State is unique in this world in that it does not require arms to win its wars. A word from the Pope can mobilize 720 million Catholics gathered from every continent. Your subjects have infiltrated everywhere, Jan Pawel, and if they wanted could provide themselves with other people's arms. Few states would be able to resist such sabotage or to destroy a fifth column controlled by the Holy See from behind the various frontiers. But the Soviet Union will never permit the solid international structures built by Marxist–Leninism to be devoured by rats gnawing at its foundations, and this is the message of which I am the bearer and which needs your immediate assurance.' Brezhnev delivered his sentences with increasing fervour. With his fists clenched on the table he appeared unable to control his agitation.

'What is happening in Poland is a direct consequence of the first phase of your pontificate,' he continued. 'In the name of religion, the Catholic Church seems intent on overthrowing the Socialist state. The Tiara you have refused in Rome you have brandished in Warsaw. This policy is leading irremediably towards the third world war!'

The Pope listened to this invective without showing any emotion, keeping his hands clasped on the table in an attitude of prayer. 'The Catholic Church does not need to plot, being conscious that, in the name of Christ, her victory will be bloodless. *Christus vincit*, for ever and ever: *Christus imperat*. Throughout her glorious history Poland has always been faithful, has overcome invasions and lacerations of every kind, against which she has fought with great courage and dignity. The Ghetto in Warsaw still echoes with the cries of the victims, exterminated while they waited in vain for the help promised them from outside. I paid the homage of the Pope in memory of those who were imprisoned in Auschwitz.'

'Let's not forget that it was Pope Pius XI and Pope Pius XII who settled the terms of the Concordats legitimizing the Nazi–Fascist regimes in Italy and Germany. The Church agreed with Mussolini in Rome and with Hitler in Berlin,' objected Brezhnev.

'If we wish to go deeper into this discussion we will be swerving from the theme you wanted to put to me. We were both silent witnesses to the pact Stalin made with Hitler to divide the spoils of a defenceless Poland. We cannot attempt to cure the ills of today by opening up the wounds of the past. You are afraid that the developments in Poland will unleash a new world war. I say again: do not be afraid.'

'The Soviet Union has amply shown its ability to triumph over the most brutal forms of oppression and intimidation. My country emerged from the Second World War victorious, with the sacrifice of more than 20 million human lives; 60,000 towns and villages were destroyed by the Nazis – a third of its natural wealth. To Pope Jan Pawel who speaks to me of groundless fears I reply with a strong appeal to common sense.'

'To praise common sense does not imply condoning the abuse of power. The Polish episcopy has been and will always be on the side of the weak and the defenceless; it has raised its voice and continues to do so against the oppressors and against the betrayers of justice. Do you think that the Pope would be able to speak with a different voice? When I was Cardinal Archbishop of Cracow I had the pleasant task of consecrating the new church at Nowa Huta. The Communist regime proposed to build Nowa Huta – a centre of a hundred thousand souls – as a town without God. The self-styled socialist culture wanted to ignore the nation's past, which counted the years of Christianity by the millennium. The new Marxist–Leninist divinity could never prevail over the one God, eternal, immortal, who watches over us all. The fifty thousand or so faithful, gathered inside and around the new church, showed that the population of Nowa Huta had resisted the propagandistic manipulation inspired by the rules of market production, and professed their identity as children of God.

The rights of man, in these circumstances, are not circumscribed by the norms of work and wages, but extend to the freedom of the spirit, to freedom of conscience, to the conviction of true religious faith. The light that emanates from the Gospels emphasizes the observance of man's rights. I do not claim that you should share this thesis. I limit myself to briefly illustrating it.' While he spoke the Pope fingered the crucifix that hung upon his breast as if to gain strength from it.

'The liberty you speak of was restored to Poland by the Soviet Union in 1945. The so-called trade unions of Solidarity, inspired and supported by the Vatican, now want to destroy social order in the name of a presumed liberty. They think that Poland has everything to gain by renouncing the socialist brotherhood and finishing up under the yoke of capitalism. He who thinks of offering the Americans Polish bases for their missiles is making a big mistake and shows his ignorance of history.' Brezhnev poured vodka into a glass and tossed it down in a single gulp. 'I drink in the hope that the militants of Solidarity return to their senses,' he exclaimed, with a semblance of heartiness.

'I know that Solidarity has made certain demands, but these demands are not for bringing back capitalism, nor for the disintegration of socialism. The workers of my country ask for a reduction in the price of essential foods, for the respect of religious practice, for freedom of association – without wanting to overthrow the structure of the State. Next to political power is the power of man. State television which denies the preaching of the Gospel also denies the value of man. Materialism cannot continue to advance at the cost of the suppression of the soul,' observed the Pope.

'The Catholic clergy and the leaders of Solidarity speak with the same voice while commemorating the incidents of 1970 at Gdansk. In order to pacify their souls the Polish Communist Party has already sacrificed its ex-leader Gierek, who was in office for a decade. Two ex-Prime Ministers – Jaroszewich and Babiuch – are in the process of vacating their parliamentary seats. At this point our Polish comrades have already done enough! No one wants to think that the agitator Lech Walesa – founder of the Solidarity movement – aspires to become a member of the Government!'

'Walesa is a worker and a good Catholic. I do not think he has any ambition to become a minister. The Church has already appealed for prudence and reason.'

'But what if this appeal fails? Behind Walesa are those agitators who preach anarchy and are always ready to act as puppets of the Pentagon. Should they become the masters of Poland – with the approval of the Church – then the Polish Communist Party will be forced to turn for help to other Socialist countries to re-establish order. In such an eventuality the Kremlin will not be able to pull back – cost what it will.'

The Pope inclined his head slightly, folding his hands together. 'You have put an apocalyptic situation before me. I can assure you, Mr President, that Christian Poland is not looking for new martyrs. The six million compatriots who fell during the Second World War are enough: one fifth of the entire population. The Catholic Church has elevated to Glory the priest Maximilian Kolbe, who sacrificed his young life at Auschwitz to save the life of another inmate who was married and the father of two children. When I knelt in front of the death cell of Father Kolbe, I described Auschwitz as the Golgotha of our times. What patriot, what sincere Christian, would wish Poland another Golgotha?'

'I hope that the distorted minds of the Polish anti-socialist agitators will be enlightened by the Pope's views. Even these elements have to remember that the postwar frontiers of Poland were established on the Oder–Neisse line thanks to the protection of the Red Army. Without Moscow's support, the Pope's native land would again have been absorbed by the forces of Nazi revanchism during the Adenauer era. This risk still holds today, and many of your compatriots give the impression of not being aware of it.'

'It was a Polish priest who, in September 1978, went to the Federal Republic of Germany to speak of reconciliation. We have Auschwitz behind us, and the graves of Katyn have not

102

yet revealed all their hideous secrets. We knelt before the cells in Dachau, which I had visited four years earlier when I was guest of Cardinal Julius Döpfner at Munich. German Christians were invited and they came to listen to me in Liebfrauendom and to seek – together with Polish Christians – the common road to justice, to peace, to reconciliation. It has been said that the history of our two peoples and the Voice of God call us towards that road.'

'The rapturous welcome you received during your recent visit to West Germany confirms that you have left happy memories behind you in that country. But the saboteurs of peace are opposed to any teaching. If the Church is not able to lead them by the sleeve before they take up arms, then the Soviet Union must chop off their hands.'

'We will never tire of teaching what is just, honourable, pure, and worthy of love. *Ecclesia docet in nomine Christi* – the Church teaches in the name of the Lord. In my land it is said that one unpleasant truth is preferable to a pious lie. This motto was quoted in June 1977 when the University of Mainz wanted to confer a doctorate, *honoris causa*, on a humble archbishop of Cracow. I think that the heads of state have to set a good example by not accepting violence as a way to peace.'

'The Soviet Union has nothing to learn in this field. The safeguarding of peace and the renunciation of nuclear armaments are constant objectives in our foreign policy. You mentioned a month which is particularly dear to me. On 16 June 1977, while you were visiting Mainz, I, as elected President of the Praesidium of the Supreme Soviet, solemnly set out to improve the living conditions of the Soviet people, to promote and strengthen peace on earth, to intensify cooperation between the peoples.'

'On that day, as on every day, I prayed for you,' said the Pope. 'As President of the USSR, you know how to value the trust of the people. No one knows better than you that to serve peace one has to respect the freedom of nations and of individuals. Without this respect, peace will always escape

103

man. I ask you, Mr President, can real peace ever exist without freedom?'

'The USSR has always recognized the indissolubility of these two precepts, which were confirmed by the Final Act of the Helsinki Conference for Security and Cooperation in Europe. I had the honour of putting my signature on that document, but many Western countries represented at that ceremony have already betrayed their commitment by following a policy contrary to the interests of peaceful coexistence. The governments of such countries do not recognize that the only alternative to peaceful coexistence would be the non-existence of their countries and of the entire human race!'

'The constant threats to peace are comparable to the fire in the bowels of a volcano that suddenly explodes, destroying man and property,' continued the Pope. 'That is why the Church never tires of preaching that the respect of freedom is a valid premise for peace. Freedom is corrupted when the rapport between peoples is based not on the respect of equal dignity but on the rights of the strongest, on the position of the dominant blocs, and on military or political imperialism. The liberty of nations is betrayed when small countries are forced to align themselves with the greater in order to secure the right to their autonomous existence or even to their survival. Liberty is corrupted when a dialogue is no longer possible between equal partners because the control of the economy is exercised by the strong and privileged nations. Peace has no real chance of survival within a country when the liberty enjoyed by every free person is not guaranteed; when all power is concentrated in the hands of one social class, of one group, or when the common good is confused with the interests of one party identified with the State.'

'These words of yours have been instrumental in fermenting the disorders in socialist countries. I am referring to the campaign conducted under the hypocritical slogan "Defence of Human Rights". Some of those who initiated this campaign claim that détente is impossible unless radical changes are

104

effected in the internal order of the socialist countries. They want to use the process of détente to weaken the socialist system and, ultimately, to secure its destruction. This tactic is presented as concern for human rights or for a so-called liberalization of the socialist system. Let us not play with words, Pope Jan Pawel, let us call a spade a spade!' exclaimed Brezhnev, getting up from his chair and nervously pacing the length of the cabin.

'The Church recognizes that true liberty is also absent when different forms of anarchy, built on theory, lead to the rejection of all State authority causing, in turn, political terrorism and blind violence – spontaneous or organized,' the Pope explained. 'At the same time there is no real freedom when the internal security of a State is invoked as the sole and supreme norm for relations between the authorities and the citizen, as if it were the only means of maintaining peace. This theory leads to systematic or collective repression accompanied by torture and murder, imprisonment and forced exile. Man, who is created in God's image, is inseparable from freedom, which no force or external restraint can ever take from him. Man is free because he possesses the faculty of self-determination and is able to recognize truth and good. To be free means having the will and the power to choose, to live according to conscience. The State, being the bearer of the people's mandate, must not only grant fundamental liberty to people but must also protect and encourage it.'

'The Soviet Union and the other socialist countries have no reason to shun any serious discussion on human rights. Our Revolution has not only proclaimed but has secured the rights of the working people, in a way capitalism has never been able to do in any country of the world. I could give you just one figure: nearly a hundred million people are at present unemployed in the non-socialist countries. Many capitalist states violate the rights of national minorities and foreign workers, the right of women to equal pay for equal work, and so on. What is the Church doing to recall those states to respect the international covenants on human rights?'

'You will have read the speeches I made during my visits to the United States, to Brazil, Mexico, Ireland, France – countries that are not under Communist control. The Catholic Church continues to raise its voice wherever injustice is perpetrated by man against man.'

'I would like your words to be understood and weighed by the propagandists of Solidarity and by the Polish dissidents of KOR, the so-called Committee for Social Self-Defence, which is pushing the country towards an economic abyss. Even the international covenants on human rights have certain limits, provided by law, which are necessary to protect national security, public order, public health and morals. Are the socialist nations expected to repudiate their laws? The Polish workers who don't want to work on Saturday pretend not to know that their country is up to its neck in debt, not only with the friendly nations of the Socialist Alliance but also with the American capitalists on Wall Street. The administrators of the International Monetary Fund have always dreamed of stretching out their hands – stained with workers' blood – to the socialist countries, and this they have partly achieved, for example in Yugoslavia. If the Polish workers' demands increase out of all proportion, the protective umbrella of the Soviet Union will no longer be enough. Neither God nor Karl Marx can coin money to pay debts. According to the latest figures, Poland has to pay back 24 billion dollars, mainly to Western governments. The American banks are owed 3 billion dollars. Prayers are not enough to balance a budget in such a bad condition.'

'I am aware of the severity of the problem. The Holy See has also had its financial problems . . .'

'. . . and if I am not mistaken, even some scandal in its administration,' interrupted Brezhnev with sarcasm.

'I do not know the details of the past but now everything is in order. Christ had to drive the merchants out of the temple because, even in those days, money exerted great fascination. Freedom is reduced in a society guided by the dogma of material increase not less than in the armaments race.

Consumption and materialism are vulgar imitations of liberty,' commented the Pope.

'Poland is assisting in this phenomenon; growing wage claims and several working reforms are unacceptable in the present catastrophic financial circumstances. The concessions granted by the First Secretary of the Communist Party, Kania, have already reached the furthermost limits. Beyond these boundaries is a pit waiting to swallow up not only the Polish nation but also mankind. We want the Pope to move before it is too late!'

'Primate Wyszynski and my brother bishops have already formulated an appeal to moderation. The Pope is associated in this appeal and will continue to be. Let us hope that the same diligence will be shown by the political regime in restoring economic equilibrium, which could be reached through the initiative of the Government. Everyone should carry out his duty in good faith. It is a road that must be followed with honesty of purpose.'

'Only those who wish to cheat reality can affirm that the Polish worker is badly treated. A Polish worker earns an average of 200 dollars a month, which is excellent pay even in capitalist countries for the same work. The average consumption of meat in Poland – according to the latest figures – amounts to 69 kg per year per head. Among countries friendly to the Soviet Union this figure is only exceeded by the Democratic Republic of Germany and by Czechoslovakia. Nobody has told us that the Polish worker is dying of hunger. Employment is guaranteed, health assistance is assured; holidays by the sea or in the mountains are subsidized by the employers . . .' Brezhnev itemized the advantages on his fingers.

'Until two years or so ago I was taking care of Polish souls. I know the needs of my people. Ten years on the waiting list for an apartment; endless queues outside food shops; twenty months' salary to buy an ordinary car – all these are still the rule. The majority of my compatriots are not asking for gold, they would be content just to have decent living conditions.'

'Comrade Gierek had planned keener competition with Western markets but did not take into account the recession and the scarcity of many products. Notwithstanding this, Poland has reached eleventh place in the list of industrialized nations. Industrial planning was a blunder and agriculture was disastrous.'

'I learned from the Polish bishops that this year's potato crop was the worst in the last twenty years, and the harvest left the country in need of at least 8 million tons of grain. Even sugar production was completely inadequate for our needs. Must we blame the weather or man's inefficiency? As you see, statistics filter through even to the Vatican,' said the Pope. 'It has not escaped us that the Finance Minister, Marian Krazk, has estimated that the increase in national income next year would be less than 1 per cent, with an increase in public spending of 22 per cent. These are likely to be painful figures for every Polish citizen, whoever he is. If errors have been made, the Virgin of Czestochowa will guide the Warsaw administrators in their search for the necessary remedies.'

'Good Polish Communists know how to practise self-criticism, but the clergy do not appear to know this type of spiritual exercise. Every national disaster is blamed by the priests on the government,' grumbled Brezhnev. 'The bitter truth that the episcopacy should impart to the faithful Catholics is quite different. The trade union disorders between July and September 1980 cost the Polish treasury a great deal. The national building industry only completed 30 per cent of its commitments in the first nine months of this year, which means that housing construction in 1980 is lacking 80,000 of the accommodation deemed indispensable. I hope the episcopacy does not ask Kania to build more churches before new houses are built, unless the Holy See has decided to turn the churches into public dormitories. Coal production was 7 per cent less than expected. I could continue, but I fear the Pope will get bored by listening to a sequence of figures.'

'Figures have their importance in the history of

Christianity. Judas betrayed Christ for thirty pieces of silver, but the freedom of man has no price.'

'Well said, Pope Jan Pawel,' reacted Brezhnev, silently applauding. 'And because figures have their importance, I am interested to know whether the 10 million members of Solidarity consider themselves to be friends or enemies of the Soviet Union. I wouldn't like to have Poland overrun by tanks in 1981.'

'I do not want ever to consider such a tragic outcome! You well know, Mr President, that this Pope will never betray his mandate as Shepherd, and that he will hasten to his flock if danger arises. Together they will withstand the tanks should Poland again be invaded. If necessary, I will not hesitate to return to my country and to share in the destiny of my people. God willing, Poland and the Church of Rome will be spared such horror.' The voice of John Paul II had become more resolute and his eyes shone with unshakable determination as he took up Brezhnev's challenge.

Rome

Yuri Andropov, as mastermind of Operation Pilgrim, personally coordinated the preparations for the secret meeting between Brezhnev and John Paul II. Before the Praesidium of the Supreme Soviet he had assumed the responsibility for the complex task of organizing the encounter, and finally saw his work go through with complete success.

The precise geographic point where the cruiser *Kirov* would stop to receive the Pope was suggested by him to the Defence Minister Ustinov after making a careful analysis of the logistic and strategic situation in the Mediterranean. A torpedo suddenly fired at the *Kirov* would have simultaneously deprived international Communism of its charismatic head and Catholicism of its spiritual leader. However, the cruiser's armed escort was such as to discourage any attack other than a ballistic missile attack which could destroy Brezhnev and the Pope wherever they were.

Andropov's main fears were concentrated on the flight of the helicopter between Castel Gandolfo and the *Kirov*, because the small aircraft would be completely exposed to the possibility of a sudden attack by land, sea or air. But who would be interested in removing John Paul II? The recent dialogues between the Christian churches made the memory of old religious wars between Catholics and Protestants fade. The Islamic, Hindu and Judaic religions were all too deeply involved in their own internal problems to contemplate acts of violence against the Polish Pope who had enthusiastically embraced the cause of ecumenism and had even inaugurated the first mosque built in Italy for a thousand years.

By a process of elimination Andropov reached the conclusion that only the Communist countries would be interested in getting rid of the Pontiff, because he had fought against Marxist–Leninism during his priesthood and episcopate in his own country – which is divided by a deep mistrust between the

Socialist State and the Catholic Church. But such a hypothesis seemed absurd when the Soviet Union – the leading country in the Socialist Alliance – had turned to the Pope in an attempt to obtain his cooperation at an international level.

These speculations reassured Andropov that Operation Pilgrim, so successfully begun, would be concluded without incident.

Only a handful of people were completely aware of what was taking place in the Mediterranean. In Moscow, as well as in the other capitals of Warsaw Pact countries, all were convinced that the Soviet President had gone to spend a few days at his dacha to rest after his exhausting official visit to India.

Together with the Minister of Defence, Ustinov, the ideologist Suslov was one of the few members of the hierarchy to be informed that Brezhnev and Gromyko had actually gone to meet the Pope.

The Soviet President had, for the period of his absence, temporarily delegated the leadership of the country to Suslov so as to ensure its continuity in the event of anything unpleasant happening to him during his journey. More than the possibility of an attack, Brezhnev feared that his illness might suddenly be aggravated while he was out of the country. Two doctors who could be trusted followed him to the Mediterranean and were sworn to secrecy about the mission, of which they knew neither the scope nor the necessity.

The crew of the *Kirov* had been told by the commander that the private visit of Brezhnev and Gromyko was motivated by the dual need for a relaxing pause from the cares of government and to supervise the consignment of relief that the fatherland of Communism had organized to help a captitalist country – Italy – after the earthquake disaster.

The arrival of the Pope and his stay on board the cruiser had been contrived to pass unnoticed by the crew.

Gromyko had left by helicopter, supposedly to inspect the 'airlift of the brotherhood' between the Soviet fleet and the provinces of southern Italy. Returning from Castel Gandolfo, the helicopter had landed on an elevator platform which had descended into the interior of the vessel before the sailors had managed to identify its occupants. Only the pilot, the copilot and the three bodyguards who had accompanied Gromyko knew the identity of the man in white. An exception had been made for the *Kirov*'s much decorated captain who, with Brezhnev, had greeted the Pope on his arrival on board.

Through the radio link installed on Capri, Andropov received the news of the Pope's arrival on the *Kirov* and the start of the discussions with Brezhnev. The head of the KGB immediately passed this information on to Suslov by telephone, using a previously agreed code. In order to inform Cardinal Casaroli of the safe arrival of the flight, Andropov availed himself of the services of the diplomat Mironov, who had already been used successfully in the organization of Gromyko's visit to Castel Gandolfo.

The headquarters of Operation Pilgrim had been set up and equipped to maintain simultaneous contact in three directions: with the *Kirov* via Capri, with the Kremlin, and with the Holy See. Naturally, Andropov had to take into consideration the danger of the Western secret services decoding at least part of the criss-cross of transmissions, in which case international public opinion would soon be aware that Brezhnev and the Pope had met under a cloak of secrecy. Such a revelation would damage the Soviet Union more than the Vatican, in that the Pope, as 'shepherd of his flock' could secretly meet with an enemy of the Catholic Church for the purpose of converting him, while a leader of the Soviet revolution would certainly arouse suspicion among his followers for holding a clandestine discussion with the head of a Christian religion, that is to say with the 'seller of opium to the people', according to Marxist doctrine. Obviously, Andropov was not prepared to consider that this meeting could be hailed by the West as an act of courageous statesmanship.

The precautions taken by the KGB to avoid a leak during Operation Pilgrim, or at its conclusion, were particularly meticulous. Andropov had carefully reexamined all the personal details of each secret agent collaborating in the

112

successful outcome of the undertaking. According to his evaluation, the only weakness in the chain was Frau Ursula Riesman, who had suddenly received orders from Moscow after having been for many years confined to Capri as a sleeping agent. The officials of the KGB had tested the capacity of the woman during her days of active service and had guaranteed her complete loyalty to the cause of Marxist–Leninism; but a long time had elapsed since Comrade Ursula – native-born German and honorary Soviet citizen for special merit – had retired into her tranquil shell. Andropov knew from experience that the use of a neglected spy could be a security risk, and he had to check two things: first, that the Capri resident had not contracted dangerous friendships or habits during her enforced inactivity, and second, that she did not learn more than she was permitted to know about the use of her house as a secret radio station. Natasha and Sergei had been ordered to prepare a report on both of these points during the first few days of their stay. This had been favourable to Frau Ursula, but Andropov was not satisfied. Proving the reliability of a woman who could betray the operation and give useful information to Western powers was too big a task to leave in the hands of his subordinates. It was therefore necessary for him to find a pretext for somebody to look her in the eye and question her closely.

On Board the Kirov (2)

The thought of Poland overrun by Soviet tanks vividly brought back to the Pope the horrors of the Second World War, with its carnage, destruction and famine.

To escape from the Nazi round-up the students of the Jagellonian University of Warsaw hid and studied in secret; the seminarists of Cracow retreated to the cellars in the archbishopric, under the fatherly protection of Bishop Sapieha. But the nightmare envisaged by Brezhnev for 1981 was even more horrifying. Forty years ago the Poles were united in the heroic fight against the invaders. This time the threat was not only from outside but included the risk of civil war, because the Soviet Union would have to use the Polish Communist Party in order to justify aggression against Warsaw before international public opinion. If the Polish Workers Party asked for military intervention from the USSR and other socialist countries, the Solidarity militants would certainly rebel against the State hierarchy and against the invaders.

The vision of his native land torn by a war of brother against brother was as intolerable to John Paul II as the idea of the Soviet Union plotting to march on Warsaw.

'Mr President, you have said things that are very serious for the future of my country. Permit me briefly to gather my thoughts in prayer: I wish to beseech Jesus Christ, *lumen gentium*, to enlighten our minds.'

'I know that when you were a young man you travelled through the countryside and the mountains carrying a portable altar on your shoulders, so that when you stopped to rest in the evenings you could pray. Our *Kirov* is equipped for this also. In the adjoining cabin I have had a kind of altar erected; it was set up by one of the crew whose parents are faithful to the Mother of God of Kasan. As you can see, we are not enemies of religion,' said Brezhnev.

114

From his travelling bag, the Pope took out the Bible and the *stola*, kissing it reverently before putting it around his neck. In the meantime Brezhnev had opened the door leading to the next cabin, narrower than the first and furnished with a bed, a wardrobe, washbasin, and a small table covered with a white cloth – the altar. On the wall above the table two crossed oars from a lifeboat symbolized the Crucifix.

'How long do you need?' enquired the Soviet leader.

'A few moments will be enough,' replied the Pope.

'I will come back in half an hour or so. Now I'll go and see that some food is prepared for us. I don't want to be accused of starving the head of the Catholic Church,' joked Brezhnev.

Left alone, the Pope knelt before the Cross and prayed. His prayers, dedicated to Jesus Christ and the Madonna, confirmed and renewed the act of consecration pronounced at Jasna Gora on 3 May 1966, on the occasion of the millennium of Catholic Poland. At the same time, he commended to Christ and to the Virgin Mary all the nations and peoples of the modern world, the brothers and sisters who were close by faith, by language, and by the destinies they shared in history, extending this consecration to the furthest limits of love, as is demanded by the hearts of a mother and of a father who embrace their children – always and everywhere.

Strengthened by prayer, John Paul II now knew how to act in order to soothe the Bear and protect Poland from its claws. When Brezhnev returned, he was sitting quietly on the edge of the bed reading the Bible.

'Pope Jan Pawel, I would like you to share a bite with me. The galley has produced several specialities of your country.' While speaking, the President of the USSR directed the Pope into a third cabin. On a wide table metal hotplates warmed bowls and dishes containing cabbage soup, paprika rice, smoked Baltic herrings, slices of chicken and turkey, dried beef à la Polenwitze; silver cutlery and porcelain plates were also set out. 'We must serve ourselves,' indicated Brezhnev, 'as the crew is ignorant of your presence on board. I lunched here today with Gromyko before he left for Castel Gandolfo. I used him as a guinea-pig to make sure the food would be acceptable to the Pope.'

'I do not doubt the excellence of the food,' smiled John Paul II, 'but I have very little appetite. I will just take a small portion so as not to be discourteous. This meeting is in danger of lasting longer than anticipated and I am expected back at Castel Gandolfo. I must return before tomorrow morning, so as to say Mass punctually.'

They helped themselves from the various dishes and then moved over to a small table laid for two. The Pope crossed himself and blessed the food before beginning to eat. As Brezhnev was about to pour wine the Pope covered his glass with his hand. 'Not for me,' he refused. 'I will just have water.'

President Brezhnev did not speak until the slices of turkey on his plate had been consumed. He leaned back in his chair, wiping his mouth on a napkin.

'I believe I have already explained that only your intervention can prevent the worst from happening. The days are numbered. If the Catholic Church does not act with the utmost urgency then the Soviet army will have to re-establish order in Warsaw. You are the only one outside the USSR to know that the Praesidium of the Supreme Soviet has decided to quell the Polish counter-revolution by force. We have been patient too long.'

'The Pope can never subscribe to the imposition of a new diktat against Poland,' replied the Pontiff. 'The Holy See has never endorsed acts of international pillage. The Church has always opposed violence with a universal, civilizing love.'

'The Vatican must not ignore the fact that Communism is also a universal church, with its own rules and its own morals. The Church preaches the brotherhood of religion; we respect the needs of a socialist brotherhood. We will not allow our Polish comrades to be crushed by the overbearing behaviour of Solidarity. I ask you to mobilize the thousands of priests and nuns in Poland to the service of peace before it is too late. In little more than a month – on 20 January next – the new American President Ronald Reagan will be in the White

House and General Haig, the standard-bearer of the Cold War, will take possession of the State Department. We want the international slate wiped clean of the Polish question as soon as possible.'

'Once again Poland is a captive nation. Do you believe that my country can be governed against the will of its workers?' asked the Pope.

'No one is asking Solidarity to give up the defence of its workers' interests. But the action of the autonomous unions has become a challenge to political supremacy, and to the guiding role of the Communist Party. Solidarity wants to become a second centre of State power, in opposition to the Government and the Party. If the unionists prefer the politics of confrontation to those of cooperation, they will receive the appropriate reply from the countries of the Socialist Alliance.'

'The Church does not preach hatred, but Christianity can never wed the Marxist ideology, which is inspired by materialism and atheism. I recall the polemics on the text of the new Polish Constitution drawn up in 1976. The Polish United Workers Party asked that the role of the "leading political force" be officially recognized. They finished up by accepting the formula of "guiding political force". But guiding to where?'

'To the construction of socialism,' Brezhnev answered at once.

'The Polish State cannot ignore the fact that more than 90 per cent of her citizens are Catholics, and largely practising. Next to the Party, which claims to be the guiding *political* force, exists the Church, and no one can deny her role of guiding *spiritual* force. This is why the Polish Constitution is held to respect the principles of human and religious freedom, while the faithful are compelled to respect State authority. It was the socialist State in the fifties that put the Primate of Poland, Cardinal Wyszynski, under house arrest. It was the same socialist State that fired on the strikers of Gdynia and Szczecin in 1970. Even the official reports at the time put the toll at 45 dead and 1165 wounded.'

'The militia only fired after the strikers had started to riot, setting fire to the Communist Party headquarters. Did the police have to wait until our Polish comrades had been burned alive?'

'I remember the slogan that circulated among the workers at Gdansk in 1970,' said the Pope. 'He who does not strike does not eat meat. It is the Polish variant of Lenin's dictum. Even ten years later, in August 1980, strikes were started because of the increased price of meat and other foodstuffs.'

'But the demands of Solidarity have assumed an essentially political nature. The *union* is posing as an opposition party and is trying to deny the participation of Poland in the world socialist system, and to sever the fraternal bond with the Soviet Union,' objected Brezhnev.

'The logic of the Yalta pact partitioning the world is revived in your words, Mr President. Poland is still considered an 'object' and not a 'subject' of international politics. The socialist State gives itself the right of promulgating laws contrary to God's laws, which it imposes on Catholic citizens. In the contest between state and religion we have always said that the Church has no intention of fighting the Communist regime. But the state cannot continue its war against religion by using the taxes of its Catholic citizens. Don't you see the contradiction? The Polish episcopy does not want to impose its teaching upon atheists and non-believers, but at the same time asks that the place it holds in society is recognized and respected in its mission and vocation.'

'Pope Jan Pawel, the dispute in Poland between the State and the Church is no longer one of philosophy, but has become political with the creation of Solidarity. During your pontifical visit to Warsaw in June 1979, you publicly embraced President Jablonski, recognizing the authority of the State. I have come to beg you to help Jablonski and his Government in removing this hotbed of subversion from the country. We ask you formally to intervene in stopping the spread of anarchy in your homeland.'

The Pope, his hands joined in prayer, thought deeply. 'I

will speak personally to the leaders of Solidarity,' he said, after a moment of silence, 'if this will serve to calm the soul of my tormented country. I will invite Walesa and his closest associates to the Vatican to give them the advice the situation requires. On your part, Mr President, I desire a formal commitment.'

'I will do everything possible in exchange for your understanding,' promised Brezhnev.

'The Alliance of the Socialist countries must give up all forms of repression against Solidarity, the religious orders and the clergy. Moderation must be unequivocal on both sides and with the same sincerity of intent. It must be done so that the future of Polish society prospers through love and not violence. I repeat the invocation of the encyclical *'Pacem in Terris'*: no war, war never again. I have entrusted the wellbeing of all Eastern Europe to the protection and intercession of the saints Cirillo and Metodio, the brother apostles of the Slavs. The Catholic Church has proclaimed them as the co-patron saints of Europe. Meanwhile, the dialogue between the Holy See and the Orthodox Church enters a decisive phase. In place of so-called armed peace, we want to substitute the peace of love that comes from God.'

'I will take your message to the Praesidium of the Supreme Soviet and to the governments of the Warsaw Pact countries. We will let Solidarity continue its activities, on the understanding that it will not attempt to transform itself into a political party. On these conditions, and only on these, will it be possible to avoid recourse to arms and the looming peril of a new world war. Next February, at the 26th Congress of the Soviet Communist Party, I will have to submit an analysis of the international situation and to render an account of the decisions made to stabilize the Polish situation. If your mediation is crowned with success it will merit the Lenin Peace Prize,' said Brezhnev, rather pompously.

'The only prizes acceptable to a Pope are those gained in the service of Christ, who is Prince and Sovereign over the nations – as is written in the Book of Isaiah. *Felix sum in servitude*,' said the Pope in Latin, which he repeated with warmth in Russian: 'I am happy in my servitude.'

The long and difficult discussion drew to a close. The fear of an invasion of Poland had been averted by the Pope with the promise that he would call upon the Polish autonomous union to exert self-control while the Soviet Union would renounce military intervention. The Soviet President felt relieved of a burden, having obtained pontifical mediation in the face of 'the saboteurs of socialism'. Now he would return to Moscow and give his report to the comrades of the Praesidum and to the leaders of other Socialist countries on the outcome of his mission and would receive the expression of admiration for this political acumen and diplomatic ability.

But was this agreement, so exhaustingly obtained, really the beginning of a long-lasting normalization of the situation or only a brief truce between the Government of Warsaw and Solidarity? History would tell.

It was almost dawn when the Pope re-entered the Soviet helicopter to return to Castel Gandolfo. Foreign Minister Gromyko was ready and waiting to accompany him to his country residence.

The meeting between John Paul II and Brezhnev had been one of emotion for both of them.

'I thank you for having answered my appeal,' said the Soviet leader, holding the Pope's hands and warmly shaking them. 'Perhaps our first meeting will also be our last, as time is running out for me.'

Their eyes met briefly and in that moment a spark of appreciation passed between them for what they had achieved. Neither one had renounced in any way his beliefs but both had clearly understood their different, deep motivations and enriched their knowledge of each other. On one point they shared the same conviction: whatever was possible should be attempted in order to prevent a new war.

The cry of the Pope, 'No war, war never again' repeated the invocation of all previous popes and their prayers, many times unanswered. Brezhnev had found in John Paul II the ready

120

reply to his own hopes. A new stage was starting for Poland and for the world: a stage of suspense, full of hope.

'I will always remember you in my prayers,' said the Pope.

'I would also like to be remembered as a good servant: a servant of socialism.'

The helicopter rose slowly over the sea, ascending into a golden, cloudless sky promising a day of sunshine.

Brezhnev remained on the deck of the *Kirov* and waved his arms in farewell. From above the Pope blessed the ship and her occupants, repeating the words of Luke: *'Gloria in excelsis Deo et in terra pax hominibus bonae voluntatis.'*

Rome

Lech Walesa, the 38-year-old Polish electrician who was suddenly the best known trade unionist in the world for having become the focus of the crisis in the Communist hemisphere, arrived in Rome on Tuesday 13 January 1981. Dark and stocky, simply dressed and with a picture of the Madonna of Czestochowa pinned to the lapel of his jacket, he has been compared with the slave Spartacus of ancient Rome – leader of the Plebs in the historical and bloody revolt against the Patricians. He had the air of a nervous and diffident tourist when alighting from the plane at Fiumicino airport.

Accompanied by his wife Danuta who, faithful to the biblical principles of 'beget and multiply' had made him a father six times, Leszek (his family nickname) was followed by a delegation of Solidarity trade unionists totalling sixteen persons, including the auxiliary Bishop of Gdansk, Klute, and three priests, among whom was the chaplain to the union, Father Jankowski.

Walesa's apparent diffidence was justified by the fact that he was venturing for the first time on a visit to a foreign country, having been heralded by a fanfare of publicity gained when he directed the strike at Gdansk in August 1980. Born into a working-class family during the Nazi occupation, Walesa was catapulted towards notoriety after having for years stubbornly tried to safeguard human and civil rights and earn for the Polish workers the chance to participate in industrial affairs.

In 1970 he was involved in the riots between the workers and the police in the Lenin shipyards. Six years later, while carrying out his duties as a union delegate, he was sacked for having dared to compile a list of grievances on behalf of his fellow workers. In 1978 he was one of the founders of a secret movement called the Baltic Free Trade Union. Dismissed twice for political activism contrary to the Communist regime, Leszek became the natural leader of the strike which produced the famous list of twenty-one reforms, known as the Gdansk Agreement, which was handed to the Warsaw Government in the summer of 1980.

With the appearance of a humble, good-natured peasant involved in events way above his head, Walesa smiled under his walrus moustache at the enthusiastic crowds gathered at Fiumicino, who applauded his arrival as though he were a conqueror.

The formal invitation to visit Rome came from the Italian unions, who are part of the General Confederation of Labour in which there is a Communist majority. The Italian union leaders, Lama, Carniti and Benvenuto, greeted the Polish guests with flowers and speeches. While the Italian unionists uttered words of welcome, Walesa's eyes were turned towards two priests who represented the Holy See: Bishop Giovanni Coppa of the Vatican State Secretariat, and the Polish Bishop Wesoly, delegate of Primate Cardinal Wyszynski for immigrant nationals. The Polish Ambassador had also sent his representatives to the airport, Counsellor Minister Rozalich and Minister Casimiro Szablewski, head of the Government delegation for permanent working contact with the Holy See.

The Vatican State Secretariat had good friends among the rank and file of the Confederation of Italian Trade Unions, from whom the invitation to Walesa and his companions had come. The Holy See immediately announced that on the occasion of the visit, the Polish trade union's delegation would also be received by the Pope, on Thursday 15 January.

Arriving in the Italian capital, Walesa did not hide the fact that the meeting with John Paul II was the most important and the most significant of all the ceremonies arranged for him during his stay.

At a Press conference, the acknowledged head of Solidarity replied to the many questions put to him by journalists with a mixture of common sense and ingenuousness that brought him further popularity from those who saw him for the first time. When he was asked whether he was at all worried about leaving Poland in a time of great uncertainty for the country, he replied:

'Life is interesting when there are many problems to be solved; if there were not life would become boring.' And when he was asked about his plans for the future of Poland he answered with peasant simplicity: 'After Monday comes Tuesday, and after Tuesday comes Wednesday.'

'What changes were there after the August strike at Gdansk?' Walesa gave another reticent answer: 'Then it was August and now we are in January.'

It was the same man who had shown no fear when climbing the gates of the factory from where he had been sacked to lead the strikers in opposing the management; it was the same man who called for the occupation of the shipyards and who demanded the immediate reinstatement of Anna Walentynovicz, a worker who had twice been decorated for military valour and who had been dismissed five months before reaching retirement age. Anna Walentynovicz was brought back to work in the factory director's car. This courageous woman was also in the delegation with Walesa in Rome.

The leader of Solidarity confessed – during his talks with journalists – to having read very few books, but added with a touch of pride: 'Seeing that I can write I must have learned to read.' He said that when having to make crucial decisions he was not guided by books but by his conscience, and added that he would go to the Pope as a son who goes to meet his spiritual father.

Walesa's own father – Stanislaw, who lived in the United States – was also in Italy's capital to embrace Leszek, but he seemed above all most anxious to meet his spiritual father, the Pontiff.

The sightseeing part of the visit to Rome and the meetings between the Polish and Italian trade unionists took place while he awaited the day of his audience in the Vatican. Speaking to a Roman labourer who asked for his autograph, Walesa confided: 'I would be a dangerous man if I were not a Catholic.'

The day before the meeting with the Pope, the delegation went to Montecassino to visit the abbey of San Benedetto; this abbey had been almost completely destroyed by bombardment and aerial attack during the Second World War, and was later rebuilt. A short distance from the abbey, among the vine-covered hills, are the graves of 1160 Polish soldiers who fell in the battle at Montecassino.

Lech Walesa and his companions prayed among the remains of their compatriots sacrificed for the freedom of Europe, and sang the national anthem that proclaims: 'Poland is not dead while we live'. The patriotic songs of the groups from Warsaw resounded even among the mosaics in the crypt of the nearby monastery: 'You, Lord, are the Defender of our Country, of our Liberty.' The invocation 'God Save Poland' recurred many times in songs and prayers that day. Mass for the guests was celebrated by the auxiliary Bishop of Danzig, Klute, and by Bishop Wesoly. A casket containing a copy of the statute of the autonomous trade union was placed among the tombs of the Polish soldiers and surrounded with flowers. This emblem of Polish renaissance was left as a tribute of affection and respect to the memory of those who sacrificed their lives in the fight against the Nazi–Fascist dictatorship.

Capri

At the onset of the Christmas and New Year festivities the island of Capri, quietly somnolent during the autumn months, suddenly wakes and puts on a different face as the visitors, escaping from the frenzied rhythm of the mainland, arrive in great numbers seeking relaxation and enjoyment of all that the island can offer of its winter charms.

The hotels, sealed in lethargy after the departure of the summer visitors, come to life for a fortnight. The porters and waiters whose services are curtailed during the winter months because of lack of work, dress themselves once again in their uniforms to welcome the arrival of the festive guests. The lights are turned on in the restaurants and ballrooms that have remained empty for the two previous months.

Even the Piazzetta is reanimated after the low season's pause, though the cold discourages visitors from sitting out in the open at the little tables lined up in front of the bars. There are some who do not fear the cold, and they can be seen swimming in the waters around the Faraglioni or in the Marina Piccola, and the local photographers are not slow in catching some bikini-clad Scandinavian intent on greedily drinking the champagne poured by her latest Latin lover to toast the New Year.

In the evenings, elderly ladies and gentlemen play bridge or poker in the hotel lounges while the younger ones dedicate themselves to dancing, nocturnal excursions, or other pastimes of a more erotic nature. Traditional suppers are prepared for the night of St Silvester – New Year's Eve – when the guests sit down to endless Lucullan courses, beginning in the early evening and ending in the early hours of dawn, when they watch the rising of the sun on the first day of January.

Itinerant musicians from the Neapolitan mainland cross the sea to perform in the restaurants and night clubs or at private villas, their engagements limited to the ten days between

Christmas and Epiphany. After Twelfth Night the students return to their schools and universities, the clerks and professionals to their respective activities, their brief interlude over.

On Christmas Eve 1980 an austere elderly gentleman installed himself in the Quisisana Grand Hotel. Professor Boris Glasunov, a Bulgarian, had, while on his way to Paestum to complete a study of the archaeological sites in the Mediterranean, decided on impulse to change course for Capri. Sitting at the hotel bar watching the barman mix a 'Sunflower' cocktail, he casually gave his reason for being on the island; the barman, not really interested, concentrated on the preparation of the drink that had won him the prize of the European Association of Producers of Alcoholic Beverages as the cocktail of the year.

Glasunov appeared very interested in local folklore and bought two tickets for a performance of the Caprese Tarantella which would be performed that very evening in the hotel ballroom after a gala supper. Frau Ursula Riesman had been invited to accompany him.

The professor had advised Frau Ursula of his arrival on Capri and had asked her to keep the evening free for him. They had never met before, but Glasunov had very good introductions from friends they both knew, and he needed Frau Ursula's assistance in finding an apartment on the island for the following summer.

Sunk in an armchair in the hotel lounge, the professor was dozing when a boy from the reception desk lightly shook his arm and informed him that a lady was asking for him. Glasunov rose and went to meet his visitor, greeting her warmly. 'At last I have the pleasure of meeting you,' he said in German.

'I have heard you mentioned many times and I am most happy that you invited me to join you,' replied Frau Ursula. She was elegantly dressed in a black silk blouse and embossed velvet skirt; a diamond brooch in the shape of a heron was pinned to the tie at her throat. They sat close together in a corner of the lounge and talked about the festivities while a group of musicians, known as the Scialapopolo, noisily performed with tambourines, cymbals, guitars, castanets, and other typically Neapolitan percussion instruments such as the *scetavaiasse*.

'I have to thank you formally for the assistance you gave to the visitors sent by the Dilecta Agency,' said Glasunov, 'though we are surprised that we have not yet received your report on their stay. The Agency is anxious to reimburse your expenses.'

'I have decided not to accept any reimbursement,' Frau Ursula replied dryly, 'and until now I have not been in the best of spirits to make out such a report.'

'Are you not well?' enquired the professor anxiously.

'I am well enough, but I believe that my loyalty to the Agency deserves something better. The couple treated me as a stupid servant, ignoring my years of service.'

'Were they impolite to you?'

'I refer to the instructions they received. If headquarters wanted to keep me in the dark about everything, why did they choose me?'

'I don't think there was anything to hide. Perhaps their visit has tired you. Why don't you have a change of scene? We would like to suggest you go on a trip – actually you may choose any place you wish.'

The noise of the band increased and the spectators clapped their hands in rhythm with the dancers.

'I have lost the urge to travel, and anyway the weather is not very encouraging.'

'In what way can we show our recognition, then?' asked the professor.

'By acknowledging my loyalty. I do not want any other form of recompense.'

'Has there been any outside curiosity for the operation on behalf of the earthquake victims?'

'Headquarters didn't display itself at its very best. Even a beginner would have guessed that the operation covered something more important.'

'For example?'

'It's not my business. I was kept in ignorance.'

'We wanted to carry out the airlift during naval exercises – that's all.'

'If you had seen the pair of them at work you would understand my reaction.'

'Have they been careless?'

'I would say they were too exuberant.'

'In their work?'

'Also . . . intimately . . .'

Glasunov nervously scratched the lobe of his ear. 'Do you think they were lovers?'

'During their stay I cancelled my domestic. I had to make the beds myself and put the rooms in order.'

'The regulations are clear. Intimate relationships are forbidden during an assignment.'

'I could be wrong . . . but then it's not my business.'

'Agreed, Frau Ursula . . . agreed. But they were under your surveillance.'

'The important thing is that they carried out their mission perfectly.'

'It was only one of simple administration.'

'You should know. I can only judge by what I saw.'

'To conclude: how would you evaluate the outcome of the operation?'

'I believe that I was an ignorant witness to an exceptional happening. But your two children overdid their duty.'

Their attention was drawn back to the musicians. Now the Tarantella had reached a giddy rhythm. The men of the Scialapopolo, in red sweaters, white breeches and green bonnets – the colours of the Italian flag – took their partners around the waist and whirled them faster and faster, their full, brightly coloured skirts swirling out about their hips like the tail feathers of a peacock. The audience applauded enthusiastically.

Glasunov sipped the wine from the second bottle of Barolo that the waiter uncorked. 'Good,' he said, 'really very good.'

129

Vatican City

The treasures of St Peter's Basilica and the Vatican Palace glowed in splendour under the dazzled gaze of Lech Walesa and his companions. The Polish electrician, his wife Danuta and the other trade unionists of Solidarity had never before seen such an awe-inspiring concentration of works of art, and were overwhelmed at the magnificent setting in which they found themselves.

Their official guide was a young priest from the Polish House in Rome; he showed them, and described, the principal features of the Basilica. Built above the tomb of the Apostle chosen by Jesus Christ as the visible head of His Church, it extends over an area of 15,160 square metres and has an internal length of 186 metres, not including the atrium and the thickness of the external walls. The imposing cupola, together with the Cross, rises to a height of 132.50 metres.

Met by priests from the pontifical State Secretariat in St Peter's Square – where they had been brought by special coach – the Polish visitors looked in wonder at the broad façade, constructed by Carlo Maderno between 1607 and 1614, before entering the Basilica down the central nave and the two flanking aisles, along which are 44 altars and 395 statues – 104 of marble, 161 of travertine, 40 of bronze and 90 of plaster. With bated breath they stood silently before the incomparable beauty of Michelangelo's *Pietà*, now under guard in the first chapel on the right-hand aisle. It was completed in 1500 when the artist was only twenty-five years old, and is the sole work to bear his signature – carved on the band that crosses the Virgin's breast. The inert body of Christ, just taken from the Cross, lies in Mary's lap. Some of the delegates of Solidarity saw in this masterpiece a symbol of a martyred Poland trusting in the maternal care of the Madonna of Czestochowa.

Walesa and his comrades slowly reached the high altar surmounted by Bernini's bronze baldacchino. The majestic

Cathedra, or Chair, made by that same Bernini during the pontificate of Alexander VII in the second half of the seventeenth century, dominates the apse. It is of bronze with gold decoration and is supported by the statues of two saints of the Latin church, Ambrose and Augustine, and by two saints of the Greek church, Athanasius and John Chrysostom. Above the bronze chair, a radiant sunburst adorned with angels encircles a dove – the symbol of the Holy Spirit and the Soul of the Church.

The visit to the Basilica on the morning of Thursday 15 January was followed by the Papal Audience. Before reaching the antechamber to the Pope's private library, Lech Walesa and his companions had to pass through many magnificent rooms where hung the testimony of at least 700 historical years of figurative art: the Clementine Room and the adjoining rooms of St Ambrose, of the Sculptors, of the Popes, of the Painters, of the Evangelists, of the Redeemer, of Our Lady, of St Catherine, of Saints Peter and Paul. Each of the names referred to a priceless painting or sculpture. The guides escorting the visitors pointed out some of the superb pieces of furniture and explained their origin.

Rectangular in shape, the Clementine Room is adorned with four allegorical figures: Charity, Mercy, Justice and Religion, and bears the coat of arms of Clement VIII, from whom the room takes its name. Walesa pondered for some time on the juxtaposition of Justice and Religion – what the Polish independent trade unions want to achieve, with the cooperation of the State authority.

The Room of St Ambrose, as the guide explained, is dedicated to the memory of the great Bishop of Milan who lived between 334 and 397; the room of the Sculptors – one of the best lit in the palace – has on display a John the Baptist by Francesco Messina; the room of the Popes – previously known as the Hall of Tapestries – contains a monument to the Eternal Father in Glory, surrounded by angels holding a mantle; the Room of the Painters derives its name from the artists, represented by a synthesis of Italian and foreign religious paintings; in the four corners of the Room of the Evangelists stand the statues of Matthew, Mark, Luke and John. In the Room of the Redeemer hangs a sixteenth-century tapestry once belonging to the Medici family and depicting Jesus meeting his Mother, but the name of the room refers to a painting by El Greco; a Madonna by Luca della Robbia hangs on the centre wall of the Room of Our Lady. The Room of St Catherine is the head office of the Prefect of the Apostolic Palace, who presides over the Pope's antechamber and controls the programme of audiences and Papal ceremonies.

On arriving in the Room of St Catherine, the Polish delegation was informed that the Pope would receive Lech Walesa first in a brief private audience. The other members of the group would be admitted to the Pontiff later.

Visibly moved by this gesture of paternal affection, Lech Walesa followed the Prefect of the Apostolic Palace through the Room of St Peter and St Paul, those great Apostles – one chosen as the Rock of the Church and the other as the Master of the early Christian community in Rome.

Finally, the leader of Solidarity crossed the threshold of the library where the Pope awaited him. John Paul II rose from the high-backed armchair behind the writing desk to meet his visitor. Walesa almost ran to him and knelt to kiss his hand, but the Pope raised and clasped him tightly in a warm embrace.

'Leszek,' he said, 'my dear son. I am so glad to see you here.' Overcome with emotion, Walesa wiped away the tears that filled his eyes as the Father invited him to sit in an armchair on the other side of the desk.

'You can tell your brother Poles that you have seen where the Pope works,' said John Paul II. 'From this table I carry out the affairs of the Church, and I can assure you that I am never short of work. This office is bigger than the one I had at Cracow, and I deal not only with the problems of the diocese of Rome but also with many other problems as well.' The rectangular writing desk had only one row of drawers, permitting the Pope to stretch out his legs beneath its surface.

On the desk was a writing pad, two pens, a carved blotter, a fine brass bracket clock, and a lamp with a white shade. On the wall behind the desk hung a painting by Antoniazzo Romano of the Madonna and Child, enthroned on a gold background and surrounded by the Apostles Peter and Paul and bishops.

Walesa had the honour to sit in the same chair as heads of state when privately received. Casting his eyes about him he could see the other furniture in the library. On either side of the desk stand two wooden carvings of prophets by a fourteenth-century German artist. In the centre of the room a fifteenth-century table holds an illuminated Bible, also of the fifteenth century. Two bookcases of the sixteenth century display a priceless collection of Bibles of different ages written in many languages, the writings of the Church Fathers, the complete collection of the Papal encyclicals, as well as several works of Church history. On the side wall hangs a crucifix in the style of Giotto flanked by two paintings by Giovanni del Biondo with saints and prophets in adoration. On the opposite side, the windows overlook St Peter's Square.

'I wish to say a few words of appreciation to you before receiving our compatriots who have followed you to Rome,' continued the Pope. 'The birth of the autonomous trade union Solidarity was a courageous act blessed by Divine Providence. But for the good of the union, and above all for the supreme good of Poland, that act of courage must now be tempered with prudence and moderation. You and your comrades, dear Leszek, must never forget the geographical, political and strategic position of our country. Do not be carried away by the enthusiasm that sometimes gives man the false impression of being invincible.'

'We have shown, Holy Father, that we are not afraid. Our Lady of Czestochowa protects and inspires us in our daily actions,' replied Walesa.

'But it is the others who are becoming afraid of what is happening in Poland. Do you understand me?'

'Who can be afraid of one who comes with his hands held

133

open in friendship?' asked Walesa. 'We have never looked for a solution through force because we are faithful, practising Catholics.'

'Listen to me, Leszek. I have heard dangerous talk of possible anarchy in the union. Someone could create a pretext to destroy what you have so painstakingly achieved.'

'No one can force us to work under the threat of arms, Holy Father.'

'I am convinced of that, Leszek, but Poland would starve if deprived of the labour of her sons. Have you considered this?'

'We are ready to relinquish anything for the good of our country.'

'You have understood exactly what I mean, Leszek. Tell your comrades that the hour has come for sacrifice; that you do not want to compromise the successes you have gained. You must resist the temptation to transform the union into something else. Resist the temptation to become a political organization more exposed to revenge and repression than the Church.'

'I understand, Holy Father; we must continue to live with our Government, even if we don't love it. But until when? We are the new Polish society and we want a government that will fulfil our hopes.'

'Remember, Leszek, that one false step could lead to tragedy. Beg your comrades to be calm, prudent and moderate. This is the message I entrust to you to take to Solidarity. Do it so that the Pope's prayers are answered.'

'If the worst happens, I will be the first to face the tanks and the last to leave the battlefield!'

'The Church has no need of Polish crusaders and martyrs, Leszek, but she has need of the faithful who know how to safeguard the peace of the country, respecting its faith and traditions.' The Pope pressed Walesa's hands as if to recharge him with a new determination.

'Do you understand me, Leszek? Do not heed the sirens of national independence. Cultivate, above everything, the independence of your conscience and be patient. Remember the examples of the other small countries near to Poland. Do not fall into the maelstrom that swept through Hungary and Czechoslovakia.'

'It is not always easy to convince my comrades, Holy Father, but you know that I will do my utmost.'

'You will see that all will listen to you when you tell them of the Pope's fears. Proceed with caution. Remove the politcal accent from the union's activities and concentrate on the labour problems. Always remember that you are not, and do not intend to be, a party but are only individuals, working for the common good. The values of the Faith are universal and cannot be restrained by the limits of a political programme. Your party is religion and does not need a label to work in the service of God. These are the recommendations that I must impress upon you!'

'I will humbly pass on your words, Holy Father,' replied Walesa. 'I assure you that we will act according to your wishes – with justice and honesty; we will be reasonable.'

Capri

On the morning of Friday 2 January 1981 Frau Ursula Riesman was found dead by her domestic when she came to the villa to do the cleaning. She was lying, fully clothed, on the neatly made bed as though she were resting. Around her everything was in order and there was no suspicion that her death was other than natural. The possibility of suicide was unthinkable, as she had never been known to suffer from depression or complained of any illness that might have led her to take her own life. The inhabitants of Via Tuoro remembered her as being a person of unfathomable character, although she was not averse to chatting about the day's events or helping to alleviate any little problem of her neighbours, or giving advice when asked.

The young students on Capri who were studying German at high school frequently sought her assistance when they had to translate some pages from Goethe or Schiller which were particularly tricky. The not so young remembered her as the tireless life and soul of evenings in the Piazzetta, of parties, of delightful gatherings in the restaurants and clubs when Capri swarmed with the affluent from every part of the world. They remembered the boutique she had run for so many years with such style as to compete with the salons of the great fashion houses on the island.

The hypothesis of murder was even more improbable, and in fact was not even considered. The doctor who examined the body immediately signed the certificate, putting the cause of death as cardiac failure. He told the woman who had found the body that: 'In such a case I would normally order a post-mortem, but no one had any reason to touch a hair of her head and nothing is missing from the house.' In the bedroom a few pieces of jewellery were neatly arranged in a small jewel case, among them the diamond heron brooch she had worn at the

Hotel Quisisana. In a drawer of the dressing table was a cheque book and about 300,000 lire in notes – the amount she had withdrawn from the bank a few days previously.

The rigidity of the body indicated that death had occurred the evening before, and the doctor suggested that perhaps the excessive eating and drinking on New Year's Eve contributed to the manner of death. But no one seemed able to say where or with whom the woman had celebrated the arrival of the New Year. In the kitchen sink two liqueur glasses and two coffee cups had been rinsed and were ready to be put away in the glass-fronted cabinet in the living room. Someone remembered that Frau Ursula had been in the habit of inviting the postman, the milkman or other delivery men in to drink a toast with her at Christmas and other festive occasions. One of them had probably been the last to see her alive.

The unpleasant task of informing the nephew of the demise of his aunt fell to the domestic, who obtained his address from an index by the telephone. He received the telegram in Wiesbaden, worded in Italian and signed by a Filomena Percuoco – a name unknown to him – advising him of his aunt's death, and saying that the funeral would take place the following day at 11 o'clock.

After having spent the last years alone, the Capri resident of the KGB went to her final Capri resting-place, escorted by a dozen or so islanders who wanted to accompany her to the burial so that she would not vanish and be forgotten like a stray dog. The nephew telephoned the Town Hall, informing whoever it was who answered that it was impossible for him to make the journey in time to participate in the funeral. He would come as soon as possible to settle the burial expenses and to begin the business of taking over the villa in Via Tuoro in accordance with his aunt's wishes.

Capri buries its dead without fuss so as not to disturb the serenity of its visitors. The sight of a coffin being carried through the narrow streets would only cause gloom to descend upon the tourist, and the thought of death is incompatible with the natural landscape, which is like a hymn to life.

Frau Ursula was taken to the cemetery early in the morning in a coffin borne on the shoulders of four Town Hall employees. The faithful who went daily to early Mass crossed themselves devoutly as the body passed, and murmured a prayer for the dead. The church service was very brief; there was barely time for a quick prayer and a benediction. She had never been seen in church and it was assumed that she had died without the solace of faith. A wooden cross with a plastic-covered card giving the name and date of the deceased pinned to it was placed on the temporary grave. No doubt relatives would provide a permanent niche.

So ended the earthly life of an obscure pawn in the Soviet secret service. A few hours before Frau Ursula's body was found, Professor Glasunov left Capri by hydrofoil, departing from the Marina Grande. He would retain pleasant memories of the island, and for some reason an emotional one also. The exploratory discussion he had with Frau Ursula on Christmas Eve convinced him that the woman was lost to the socialist cause. The resentment she harboured against headquarters made her unreliable and probably irretrievable. He sent his report to Yuri Andropov couched in these terms and awaited further instructions.

The verdict condemning the KGB ex-resident of Capri was communicated to Glasunov on 31 December, and gave him two days to complete the assignment. The professor telephoned the woman telling her of his forthcoming departure and saying that he would like to pay a short farewell visit.

On the evening of 1 January, Frau Ursula received her last guest at the villa in Via Tuoro. They conversed quietly together, and the visitor assured her that he would certainly endeavour to do what he could with headquarters to dispel all the misunderstandings derived from Operation Pilgrim. Ursula Riesman had no reason to doubt the appreciation that the organization had of her ability, fully demonstrated during her many years of service. Even the most brilliant agent of the KGB has moments of stagnation that could mistakenly be interpreted as a prelude to oblivion. In the game of chess it sometimes happens that essential pawns are held back the better to plan an attack against the adversary.

While listening to these comforting words Frau Ursula had offered her visitor something to drink. Focusing their attention on the port bottle, they filled their glasses and sipped the heady wine. Glasunov told her that his next assignment would take him to Turkey. Later, he suggested that she make a pot of Neapolitan coffee for him, after learning that she had the correct blend and the correct type of pot. Ursula went into the kitchen leaving her guest admiring some pieces of Dresden china which decorated the lounge.

The professor exaggeratedly praised the steaming, fragrant liquid served to him by Frau Ursula. He mentioned the aniseed coffee he had tried in Naples and went on at length on the merits of the *sambuca* of Civitavecchia. When Frau Ursula suddenly fell back in the chair clutching at her stomach with both hands, Glasunov did what he could to help her. He thought it best to get her to bed, and with difficulty dragged the inert body up the stairs. When he realized that there was nothing further to be done for her, he made sure the house was in order before leaving. He carefully washed the cups and glasses with a special detergent powder he carried in a small container in his pocket. In closing the front door behind him, he gave a slight bow as though Frau Ursula was just inside the threshold saying goodbye. If anyone from the street had seen, they would have been convinced that at that moment Ursula Riesman was still alive.

In the Hall of the Consistory

At 11.30 on the morning of Thursday 15 January 1981 Pope John Paul II, after having privately spoken with Lech Walesa, granted an audience to the Polish delegation of Solidarity in the Hall of the Consistory. The meeting took place in the presence of numerous members of the Polish community resident in Italy, and of journalists from many countries.

Speaking in Polish, the Holy Father gave a discourse, the whole context of which, in the circumstances, merits reflection by the readers of this book.

The following is a free English translation of the entire text. All the words given in italic type in this translation were underlined by the Pope himself in the original Polish text.

Praise be to Jesus Christ!

1. I express joy at today's visit of the representatives of Solidarity – Poland's autonomous trade union – and cordially greet Mr Lech Walesa and all those who accompany him. I am happy that the head of the Polish Government's delegation for permanent working contacts with the Apostolic See and his colleagues are also taking part in this meeting.

   I greet you with particular warmth here, where, because of my ministry, I have the opportunity of meeting men and women of different nations, tongues, races, countries and continents – *with mankind: with my brothers*. This universal brotherhood of man – which the Church proclaims in the name of Jesus Christ and in the context of the whole gospel message – this brotherhood that unites sons and daughters of the same nation has a special place and special right, because it still has a special place and right in man's heart.

   I greet you, therefore, as my fellow countrymen, to whom I am bound by the ties of language and culture, of common history and experience, through which *the solidarity of all Poles* was formed over the centuries – a solidarity revealed above all in times of difficulty and crisis throughout the history of our country.

2. I rejoice in the fact that the events of last autumn, which began in those memorable weeks of August, have been the means of showing that same solidarity, which attracted the attention of public opinion all over the world. Everyone stressed the *maturity* that Polish society, and particularly the Polish working man, showed in undertaking and solving the difficult problems that have come about at a critical time for the country. Against the background of violence and arrogance, even terror, that so often mark events in the world today, this *way of acting*, free from *violence and arrogance*, seeking solutions through dialogue and bearing in mind the common good, is a credit both to labour leaders and to the State authorities in Poland.

I would like to assure you – although I am sure you are already aware of it – that during this difficult period I have been with you in a special way – above all in prayer, but also occasionally by acting in a fairly discreet manner that at the same time was sufficiently comprehensible to you and to all men of good will.

3. I learned with joy that through the *approval of the statute of the free union Solidarity* of 10 November 1980, the union became the organization authorized to carry out its work in our native land. The creation of a free union is an event of great importance. It indicates the readiness of all working men in Poland – including those of the professions, the 'white collar' workers and the farmers – to undertake joint responsibility for the dignity and fruitfulness of work carried out in our native land. It shows, too, that there is no contradiction between such an initiative and the structure of the system which refers to human work as well as to the fundamental value of the life of society and the state.

Work is the labour of man. It is his conscious and personal activity, his contribution to the great achievements of past generations, the preservation and the progress of humanity, of nations, and of families. It is clear that men who carry out a certain job have *the right freely to form associations precisely on account of this*, to ensure the benefits derived from such work.

It is a question of the fundamental rights of the individual, the right of man, as the specific subject of work, who, 'subduing the earth' (in the words of the Bible) through work, wishes at the same time that, in the sphere of work, life 'should become really human', as we read in the texts of the last Council.

4. The trade unions have a fairly long history in the countries of Europe and elsewhere in the world. The Polish unions also have their history. This was mentioned by the Primate of Poland, Cardinal Wyszynski, who is an expert in union problems in the period between the two world wars, in his address after the approval of your statutes.

5. I think, ladies and gentlemen, that you are fully aware of the duties that are in store for you in Solidarity. These are of enormous importance. They are connected with the need for a full guarantee of the dignity and efficacy of human endeavour, which means respect for all the personal, family and social rights of man. In this sense these duties have a fundamental significance for the common good of the whole of society. After all, the common good can be reduced to the question: who makes up society; how does he live and work?

Therefore your independent activity is, and must always be, clearly linked to the whole of social morality. First of all to the morality connected with work, to relations between the worker and the employer; but also to other fields of morality: personal, family, environmental, professional and political. I think that at the base of that great initiative of yours there was a collective effort to raise the morality of society. Without this we cannot even speak of any real progress. And Poland has the right to real progress – the same right as any other nation. At the same time, in a certain way, it has a special right, earned by the great trials of history, most recently by the sufferings of the Second World War.

6. It is and will continue to be a close internal problem for all Poles. The efforts of those autumn weeks were *not* directed *against anyone*, nor are the enormous efforts that still continue to confront you. They are not directed against . . . *but exclusively towards the common good*. To undertake such an endeavour is a right – no, more, a duty of every society, of every nation! It is a right reconfirmed by the whole international code of life. We know that in the course of history the Poles have been deprived, more than once, of this very right. This did not, however, make us lose our faith in Divine Providence or our habit of starting all over again. It is in the interests of peace and the international juridical order that Poland should fully enjoy this right. World public opinion is convinced of the reasonableness of this position.

   The activity of the unions *does not have a political character* and must not be an instrument of the conduct of anyone or of any political party, so that it can concentrate exclusively and with complete freedom on the great social good of human endeavour and on the welfare of working people.

7. At our meeting today I desire, my dear guests, to give you my best wishes. These are many, but there are two in particular:

   In the first place, my wish is that you will be able, in peace and with constancy, to continue your activity, which is dictated by such important social motives, letting yourselves be guided by justice and love and the good of our country.

   My second wish is that you always have the same *courage*

that you had at the beginning of your initiative – and also the same *prudence* and *moderation*.

The good and the peace of our country demand this, as Cardinal Wyszynski pointed out in the address I mentioned, and on other occasions. When you undertake this task, which you yourselves have consciously chosen, try to render an historic service for the good of our country and also for all the nations of the world.

This is what I wish for you, and I will not cease to pray to God for it through the intercession of Our Lady of Jasna Gora, Mother of the Poles.

Vatican City

The Pope wanted to give a further sign of paternal kindness to Lech Walesa and the delegation of Polish trade unionists before their departure from Rome. On the morning of Sunday 19 January, the group from Warsaw attended Holy Mass in the private chapel of the Papal apartments. The rites were celebrated by the Holy Father, assisted by the Auxiliary Bishop of Gdansk, Monsignor Klute, by Monsignor Wesoly of the Polish House in Rome, and by the Polish priests of the Church of Saint Bridget at Gdansk.

The guests were ushered into the chapel a few moments before 7 o'clock and so had an opportunity, while awaiting the Pope's arrival, to study their surroundings. The chapel is a precious jewel of figurative art put to the service of religion. Rectangular in shape, it was designed and built by Dandolo Bellini, and though small in scale is sufficiently spacious to offer the Pontiff a place of seclusion in which to pray and meditate whenever he desires. The simplicity of the architectural line is perfectly in harmony with the restraint of its decoration, creating an atmosphere conducive to a silent dialogue between the Vicar of Christ and the Supreme Being represented by him on earth.

The altar, which faces the entrance to the chapel, is supported on columns decorated with three sculptures by Enrico Manfrini representing Pentecost, the Annunciation, and the Assumption of the Virgin. A simple crucifix, also by Manfrini, dominates the altar. The tabernacle – a work by Luigi Martinotti – is surrounded by branched candlesticks, and is engraved in enamel representing praying angels. On either side of the altar, two mosaics by Silvio Consadori represent the martyrdoms of St Peter and St Paul; at the four corners of the chapel stand the statues of Manfrini's Evangelists.

The floor and the walls are of coloured marbles and on the ceiling, painted by Luigi Filocamo, the three-dimensional figure of the Risen Christ is surrounded by angels.

The Pope's prie-dieu, set before the altar, is the work of the sculptor Mario Rudelli; this, and the Chair, are decorated with carvings symbolic of the arts and crafts, and also with pelicans and peacocks by a fountain. The side wall panels depict scenes from the Passion by Lello Scorzelli. The bronze door leading into the chapel is by Enrico Manfrini and shows the Graces. Two sculptures, one of the Baptism of Christ and the other of the Queen of the Angels, stand at either side of the entrance. Above the altar, stained-glass windows illustrate scenes from the Old Testament.

In this atmosphere of spiritual concentration, cut off completely from external noise, the popes prayed in moments of grave international crisis for the peace of the world and for the salvation of mankind. The exceptional welcome shown by John Paul II to the Polish delegation attending Mass had special significance, which reached its peak when the Pope personally administered the Sacrament of the Eucharist to Lech Walesa, to his wife, and to his companions.

During the celebration of Mass the Holy Father delivered a sermon offering new and profound sources of inspiration. He quoted the words of the Evangelist: 'I come, Lord, to do Thy bidding', invoking the image of Christ on the banks of the Jordan at the beginning of his Mission, which was to do the Will of the Father. John the Baptist pointed to the Saviour saying: 'Here is the Lamb of God who will take away the sins of the World.' And the Voice of God responded from on high: 'This is my dearly beloved Son, in whom I am well pleased.'

The Liturgy – explained the Pope – confirms the revelation of Jesus Christ on the banks of the Jordan, and we participate in this revelation as the manifestation of the vocation of man in Jesus Christ. 'As I begin the Liturgy of the Sacrifice of the Lamb of God, all of Poland comes into mind, dear brothers and sisters – the Poland in the field of work, the field of human endeavour, of Polish labour; I refer to physical and mental work – to the work in the factory – and to the work of ordinary people; to the work of the family, to the work of mothers and fathers. Today, I welcome you, pilgrims and representatives of

Solidarity, and through you I can see the enormous task you are carrying out in our native land. I want, before you and together with you, to reunite at this altar all the people of Poland, to offer up the bread and the wine for all that is contained in the daily life of Poland.'

The Pope continued: 'I beg you to offer up – here on the altar of the Pope's chapel – this Polish work, symbolized in the bread and the wine. Our sacrifice becomes the Sacrifice of Jesus Christ, of the Lamb of God. The mystery of the Jordan is repeated here, before this gathering. We can hear, thanks to the inner voice of faith, the words of the Father: "This is my dearly beloved Son, in whom I am well pleased." And He, the Son of God, will give us strength. In offering up on this altar all our Polish labour, the strength that flows from Him will enter our souls and the souls of those we represent – to all who labour for our Polish land; this strength that makes man the Son of God and grants him dignity throughout his life and work.'

The Pope concluded, saying: 'Dear brothers and sisters, in offering this sacrifice we pray that Solidarity – the solidarity of all the workers of Poland – will be used in this great cause. I beg you to take these words with you – the words of your compatriot, of the Successor of Peter in the Apostolic Chair, and to repeat them to the workers of Poland: that their work is for the dignity of humanity, elevating man, elevating the family, elevating the people.'

The sermon given by the Pope in his private chapel and his speech in the Hall of the Consistory were perfectly integrated in a paternal appeal to the Polish nation, and in particular to the workers of Solidarity, that they might be prevented from taking any reckless step.

In exalting the three theological virtues – faith, hope and charity – the Pontiff invoked a further three virtues – courage, prudence and moderation, which his compatriots would have to practise assiduously to enable them to emerge from the crisis unharmed.

To the courage shown by the militant autonomous trade unions in challenging the monolithic organization of power in

147

the socialist countries must now also be added renunciation and sacrifice. They should refrain from any confrontation with the State authorities leading to a complete break, which would have bloody consequences, and show sacrifice through working towards the improvement of the economic situation. An allegorical interpretation of the sermon conferred Poland with the role of the 'Lamb of God' sacrificed on the altar for the supreme good of peace.

Solidarity was the dearly loved Son of whom the Father had reason to be well pleased.

The sixth point of the speech directed at the Polish pilgrims in the Hall of the Consistory had stressed the fundamental concept of the mediatory and restraining intervention of the Pope. 'The efforts of those autumn weeks,' he had said, 'were *not* directed *against anyone*, nor are the enormous efforts that still continue to confront you. They are not directed against . . . but *exclusively towards the common good.*'

The words in italics were underlined by the Pope himself in his original manuscript, and therefore have a special significance. For the first time the Pope had inserted dots in his speech leaving words unsaid, so that each of his listeners or readers could fill in the space according to his understanding. He wanted to say that the revolt of the Polish workers was not against anyone, including in this 'anyone' the Soviet Union and other socialist countries. Reading the translation of the speech, Brezhnev would have confirmation that the Pope was using his enormous influence to calm the souls of the 'rebellious' Poles.

At the termination of the Mass, the Pope asked his guests to follow him to the refectory in the Papal apartments, and to sit with him around the oval walnut table to eat breakfast together. The Polish sisters of the Sacred Heart – who were in charge of the domestic management of the Pope's household – had set the table lavishly with an embroidered cloth and napkins of Flanders linen, with silver dishes and delicate French porcelain. According to Polish hospitality, plates of cheese and ham sandwiches, smoked herrings, eggs – pickled and hard boiled – were set out, next to the jams and honey, the tea and the coffee. The Pope's meals were always frugal, but in honour of his guests the nuns had prepared more than usual.

But the food and drink were only a way to prolong the time before the Pope parted from his well-beloved children, each one of whom was asked about his family and way of life. Later, the old popular songs of Poland resounded in the room, and John Paul II joined in the choruses. They would have remained with the Pope all day if he had not brought them back to the reality of the present. 'I know that you must leave and I am sorry I cannot keep you with me longer. Perhaps it is for the best, because these songs bring back to the Pope moving memories, and he does not wish to weep.' They crowded around him for the last spiritual embrace.

The exchange of gifts between the Pontiff and the delegation also acquired a symbolic meaning. The visitors gave the Pope a reproduction of the monument to the workers who fell at Gdansk on 16 December 1970 and a medallion commemorating the tenth anniversary of that tragic event, an album containing photographs of the Mass celebrated during the strike at Gdansk in August 1980, and an advance copy of the magazine *Solidarity*, not yet published. With particular emotion the Pope received from the hands of Lech Walesa a casket containing a handful of earth from Shuttow, near Gdansk, where there had been a concentration camp during the Second World War, a handful of earth from Westerplatte, in memory of the Nazi invasion of Poland, and another handful of earth taken from the ground where the workers of Gdansk were killed in 1970 and where, ten years later, a monument to their memory was erected.

The Pope gave each visitor a medallion of his pontificate, a rosary, the Polish text of the message for the Day of Peace in 1981, and a copy of the speech he had delivered in the Hall of the Consistory.

Immediately on his return to Warsaw after the visit to the Vatican, Lech Walesa was received by the Prime Minister, Josef Pinkowski, and was held in discussion for four hours in his capacity as President of the National Committee of

149

Solidarity. The conversation was conducted in a climate of hope for the solution of the crisis.

Twenty days later, on 10 February 1981, Pinkowski was replaced in office by General Wojciech Jaruzelski. Formally proposed by the Polish Communist leader, Stanislaw Kania, the nomination of Jaruzelski, a man loyal to Moscow and an exponent of the military alliance of the Warsaw Pact, was unanimously approved by the Polish Parliament, Sejm, with only two abstentions. Already Minister of Defence for more than thirteen consecutive years, Jaruzelski has retained that office, combining in one person the direction of both civil and military affairs in Poland.

Rome

'I have been asked, on behalf of the Praesidium, to thank officially all those who took part in Operation Pilgrim, and I wanted you to be the first,' said Yuri Andropov.

Sergei and Natasha stood before him like students summoned into the presence of the school principal to receive their end-of-term report.

'The transport of Soviet aid to the earthquake areas of southern Italy has been completed without incident – which is partly due to your efficient radio contact with the fleet during the most delicate moments of the operation,' added the head of the KGB, with good humour and winking an eye. From his desk he took two boxes and two envelopes, on each of which was written the name of the recipient. 'I am very happy to tell you that the Order of the Red Flag has been conferred on both of you. Together with this honour you have also been promoted, which means, as you know, transfer to new posts. Detailed instructions are contained in these envelopes, which you should study privately according to service regulations. After deciphering the instructions and committing them to memory, you each have the responsibility of destroying them. I am leaving Rome in two hours and I still have one or two things to get through. I want to congratulate you on the success of Operation Pilgrim and on the further progress of your careers.' Having said this, Andropov took a bottle of Asti Spumante from the refrigerator in the office. 'When in Rome, drink as the Romans drink!' he laughed, unwiring the foil-covered cork. 'Have you anything to tell me?' he enquired, handing them each a glass of the sparkling wine.

Natasha and Sergei looked at each other in surprise and with a vague feeling of apprehension. 'I am only sorry that Frau Ursula is not with us. Official recognition of her efforts would have made her very happy,' said Natasha.

'Poor thing,' murmured Yuri Andropov, shaking his head sadly. 'I have received a copy of the medical certificate. It was a heart attack. No one told me she was ill.'

'She did not appear to be ill,' commented Sergei. 'She was an active woman – full of energy.'

'It must have been the emotion at finding herself for the first time in the middle of a very important mission,' opined the head of the KGB.

'Let us drink to her memory!'

When the time came for goodbyes Andropov embraced Natasha and Sergei warmly and patted them energetically on the back. 'I know you will continue to distinguish yourselves in your new posts. Good luck, comrades. Until next time. You can always count on me as a friend.' He escorted them to the door of the office with a smile on his lips.

Natasha and Sergei met that same evening in front of the Palazzo Farnese.

'Peking,' hissed Sergei, as soon as she was close to him.

'Moscow,' replied Natasha.

'Are you happy?'

'How could I be? Do you realize that we will be parted for ever?' Her eyes were red, more with anger than with tears. 'Andropov wants to separate us! We may never see each other again – now that you are posted to Peking!'

'I don't think so. One is frequently called back to Moscow for talks.'

'Only if headquarters think it is necessary.'

'Yuri said we can consider him our friend. He wouldn't refuse me a trip to Moscow every three months.'

'Would that satisfy you?'

'We have to play the game according to the cards we hold. We have no other choice,' said Sergei. 'I am beginning to learn something of Italian fatalism.'

'I don't wish to surrender myself to fate.'

'Do you wish to jeopardize your career, then? Transfer to Moscow will put you right in the midst of everything – you should be proud. After all, you have been promoted.'

'I have been assigned to the Chief's personal secretariat, without a scrap of freedom. This is not what I was hoping for.'

'I thought you had grown out of the age of dreams. What are you thinking of doing, then?'

Natasha cosidered a moment before answering. 'I am not sure yet, but I don't think I want to go back to Moscow while you are sent out to some remote place such as Peking.'

'You are talking like a foolish child. You know very well we have work to do.'

'Work . . . and then more work! To end up like Frau Riesman, thrown out on the rubbish heap!'

'Don't compare yourself with Riesman.'

'Her death has taught me many things. I see myself in her place, old and alone, after having sacrificed her entire life for the service. And then, at a certain moment, she was considered useless – like an old rag.'

'You will always be useful – here the comparison ends,' Sergei said placatingly.

'They use us as though we were amorphous things. I refuse to be treated like a robot!'

'It's certainly true that Italy is the country of melodrama,' commented Sergei dryly.

Holding hands, they crossed the bridge over the Tiber. The mass of Castel Sant'Angelo rose up in front of them, the great battlements of the ancient fortress reflected in the water of the river. Scows and barges were moored to posts and some youths were kicking a football on the gravelly river bank.

'Will you be sorry to leave Rome?' asked Sergei, looking about him at the buildings silhouetted against the purple sky.

'This city gets into the blood and the memory of it lies under the skin. But it is something else – and you know it.'

'You don't imagine that it's easy for me,' admitted Sergei.

'I don't know what to hold on to – now that I have lost all enthusiasm for my work. Your situation is different. You have your sons and a wife.'

Sergei was becoming irritated by the conversation. 'My sons will grow up and go away, but my career will remain. I was always under the impression that not marrying was your own choice.'

'So it was, that's true, but I am beginning to doubt my decision. When you have always built for others, you suddenly become aware of having built on nothing – of being in a vacuum.'

'And love of country? You seem to have forgotten it.'

'Long live the patriotism that denies me my happiness,' cried Natasha bitterly.

'You mustn't be unhappy. We will see each other again soon. Anyway, we have not been parted yet.' They had walked down the Via della Conciliazione and were slowly going towards St Peter's Square.

'Let us go and pay homage to the one who enabled us to meet again,' proposed Sergei, jokingly.

'I would have preferred not to have met you again.'

'But why?'

Instead of answering, Natasha bit her lip, holding back the tears. Sergei drew her towards him and held her close. They were now in the centre of the square, in front of Bernini's colonnade. The lights in the third loggia of the Apostolic Palace were burning, and indicated that John Paul II was still at work.

Sergei tried to bring a smile back to her trembling lips. 'Stalin always left the lights on in his study to make people think that he was tirelessly at work. Mussolini did the same in the Palazzo Venezia. Do you think the Pope also plays the same trick?'

'I now know enough about him to think not.'

'You aren't by any chance being converted to Catholicism?'

'Don't be a fool. Admiration has no racial or ideological limits.'

'Like love,' added Sergei.

'You have never spoken of your feelings for me.'

'I prefer the act to the word.'

'You will give up neither your career nor your wife to stay by my side,' she flung at him angrily. These words hit Sergei like a slap in the face.

154

'In affairs of the heart, I know I'm a swine,' he admitted.

'You could have done something to stay with me but you didn't . . . I would have done anything to remain near you – what a fool I was!' Freeing herself from his arms, Natasha ran to where taxis were lined up on one side of the square waiting for hire. Recovering from the first amazed shock, Sergei tried to catch her, but she had already jumped into a cab and was speeding away out of the square. He decided not to follow her. It was better to leave her alone for a while – to give her time to calm down and come to her senses. The instructions he had received ordered him to leave within two days and to make contact with the Embassy in Peking.

Instead of returning to the small block of apartments in Via Salaria – entirely occupied by Soviet diplomats – where she lived, Natasha sought refuge with an old lady who had taught her the rudiments of Italian when she first arrived in Rome. They had remained good friends and saw each other frequently. During last summer they had shared a bathing cabin on the beach at Fregene. She knew that her friend would have a room and not ask questions, but to explain her sudden visit she had the excuse that her apartment had just been redecorated and the smell of paint would make sleeping there impossible.

She passed the night reflecting upon her future. She had made a big mistake in thinking that her attachment to Sergei would triumph over all obstacles. She now realized that Sergei did not return her love with the same intensity – perhaps he had never really loved her at all. If she returned to Moscow, following the orders she had received, she would have to give in to the demands of Andropov or face up to his anger and resign herself to his revenge. The third way open to her was defection, although she did not totally deny the ideology which she had so wholeheartedly and conscientiously served or the work she had accomplished. She was suddenly confused, disillusioned.

The following morning Sergei tried to contact Natasha at the Embassy in Via Gaeta but without success. She had not been to the office, and the Soviet caretaker of the apartment block in Via Salaria ascertained that she had not come home the previous night. The alarm went out immediately to hospitals and the police but without success.

Excluding the possibiity of a fatal accident or amnesia, which would already have been discovered, it must be presumed that Natasha Ranskolnieva had found asylum in a Western country. But where?

Epilogue

On 7 January 1981 the Italian Government ordered the expulsion of the Soviet diplomat Anatoli Zazouline, commercial attaché to the Soviet Embassy in Rome. This name has not been mentioned in the preceding pages, which refer to a period when Zazouline was, presumably, occupied with the clandestine operations for which he was designated *persona non grata* and forced to make a hasty departure. The trade of espionage is full of chameleon-like figures, of mysterious and hidden connotations, of people working in the shadows who suddenly vanish, sometimes to reappear in a different and unsuspected guise.

On the afternoon of 13 May 1981 a sacrilegious hand was raised against the Pope. The echo of the four shots fired at His Holiness in St Peter's Square – crowded with pilgrims – shocked and horrified the world. Speaking of this act, the Secretary of State, Cardinal Casaroli, said that the incredible attempt had written an unforgettable and bloody page in the 2000-year history of Christianity.

Mehmet Ali Agca, twenty-three-year-old Turk and would-be assassin, initially told the police and investigating magistrates that he had acted alone, without instigation or help from abroad, and that his sole purpose was to kill the Pope. The weapon used for the crime was a 9-calibre Browning brought in from outside Italy. Investigations into the sniper's turbulent past were made in an endeavour to find some trace of complicity.

Until the end of 1977 Agca had been in contact with both left- and right-wing extremist organizations. He was sentenced to death by default in his own country for the murder, motivated by ideological hatred, of a journalist. While awaiting sentence he escaped and fled abroad. Reconstruction of his movements, although confused and inexact, show that he was certainly in

Iran, Tunisia and Germany before going to Italy with the intention of ending the life of the Pontiff.

The hypothesis of a plot against the Pope was voiced for the first time – in the restrained terms of diplomacy – on 29 June 1981 by Cardinal Casaroli. During Mass in celebration of the Feast of Saints Peter and Paul, while John Paul II was still lying in hospital, the Secretary of State spoke to the congregation, saying: 'A hostile heart has armed an enemy's hand to strike at the very core of the Church through the Pope – this Pope – to try and quench a voice raised solely to proclaim truth, to preach love, and justice, and peace.'

If there was a plot, who masterminded it? Who armed the profane hand of Mehmet Ali Agca? Investigations showed several possibilities directly pointing towards those governments and regimes whose intention it is to sabotage any peaceful attempt at overcoming the Polish crisis. The possibility of a 'Bulgarian Connection', strongly denied by the Sofian authorities, was put forward by the Italian Government at the end of 1982, following upon a later admission made by Mehmet Ali Agca.

It is obvious that the prospect of a regenerated and stabilized Poland – coming from the birth of the independent trade unions – has spread fear throughout Eastern Europe, now exposed to the risk of ideological counterblows and to the possibility of the 'centrifugal contagion' that would develop.

The events set out in this book preceded by only a few months the shooting in St Peter's Square, and could perhaps offer a key to solving this enigma. The posthumous revenge of Frau Ursula against the KGB for their lack of trust in her was probably achieved by her sending a betraying communication to a receptive body in the weeks between Operation Pilgrim and her death on Capri.

This 'receptive body' could be found only in one of those countries that had a strong interest in preventing the survival of Solidarity. To name the secret service receiving the German spy's message would be tantamount to attributing it with complicity or even with masterminding the attempt on the life of Pope John Paul – but without any legal corroboration. The reader must, therefore, draw his own conclusions according to the evidence that is only now beginning to emerge.

Exactly six months after the failed assassination attempt (13 December 1981) the Government presided over by General Jaruzelski imposed martial law in Poland. Further horrors and repressions have befallen this lovely country, which was first crushed in the mortal embrace of the Soviet Union and of Nazi Germany on the eve of the Second World War, later torn apart by the frontal encounters between the Third Reich and the Red Army, and finally consigned to the undisputed domination of Moscow according to the agreement reached by the great powers at Yalta.

And the 'Black Madonna' continues her silent vigil on the destiny of a European people condemned to an interminable martyrdom.

It would be useless to ask the author if Frau Ursula was converted to the double game *in articulo mortis* or had been a double agent for some time; it would also be useless to ask him the whereabouts of Natasha, for he does not know, and if he did he would never tell you. Gorgias the Sophist put the question: 'What is truth but what we believe to be truth?'